TRAVELS OF
WILLIAM ALEXANDER
THOMSON,
1842-1844

Kenneth MacRitchie

Photograph of William Alexander Thomson, from the Parliament of Canada Biography. Public domain. Date and photographer's name not provided.

Contents

EDITOR'S PREFACE

William Alexander Thomson (1816-1878) was a Scottish-born Canadian railroad entrepreneur and legislator. He was also my great-great-grandfather. His mansion, Glencairn, is on the Ontario side of the Niagara River, just downstream from Queenston. Glencairn is a large white wedding-cake structure. It passed out of the family shortly after his death, and remains in private hands. His burial plot is at Saint Mark's Anglican Church, Niagara-on-the Lake, Ontario.

In 1842-1844, William A. Thomson traveled from Buffalo, through the Eastern Seaboard, then to England, Ireland, and Scotland, then back to Buffalo. He left a manuscript describing his experiences. In the United States and Canada in the Nineteenth Century, there were any number of industrialists of the Scottish diaspora. This manuscript enables us to get inside the mind of an industrialist of the Scottish diaspora

Manuscript Provenance

William A. Thomson's manuscript must have been a handwritten manuscript, because typewriters didn't exist in 1842-1844. His granddaughter Dr. Mary M. Thomson (1892-1985) had a typescript version, which she gave to my mother Helen E. (Fellowes) MacRitchie (1923-2013). My mother left the typescript version in her estate. The handwritten manuscript version has been lost.

Editorial Arrangements

The typescript version of the manuscript contained no chapter divisions; I divided the work into chapters and assigned chapter titles. I also standardized the spellings, and eliminated eccentricities of capitalization and punctuation.

The footnotes are all my own. After I entered the typescript on my computer in Microsoft Word, I did Google searches to identify the various places, persons, and events described by William A. Thomson; these ended up as footnotes. When I did these Google searches for the footnotes, I found that almost everything checked out: ship names, cities and towns, natural geographical features, governmental bodies, buildings, monuments, personal names, company names, literary works, and events. The only thing that did not check out was the Court of Rolls in London (no such court).

To thicken the plot, the typescript version of the manuscript, as left in my mother's estate, actually came in two nearly identical variations, each approximately 100 pages long, which I dubbed Variation A and Variation B. When I entered the typescript on my computer in Microsoft Word, I harmonized Variation A and Variation B.

Both Variation A and Variation B of the typescript manuscript contain two gaps, which occur at the same places in both variations, and which probably resulted from missing pages in the handwritten version of the manuscript. The first of these gaps is in Chapter 4, and the second is in Chapter 16. These two gaps were probably short: before and after the gap in Chapter 4, we are in Stranraer; before and after the gap in Chapter 16, we are in London.

My relatives on the Thomson side of my family always regarded the travels of William A. Thomson as a continuous journey. Looking at the dates scattered throughout the typescript, there is a separation of one and three-quarter years between leaving Connecticut (February 26, 1842) and embarking on a ship for England (November 25, 1843). Thus, the typescript is probably the combined narrative of two separate journeys.

Historical Background

When William A. Thomson visited Great Britain, Queen Victoria had been on the throne since 1837, and had married Prince Albert in 1840. The first of the three Reform Bills had been enacted in 1832. The Irish potato famine would begin shortly in the future, in 1845. Sir Robert Peel had started his second term as Prime Minister in 1841, and would remain in office until 1846. In the United States, the Panic of 1837 caused widespread economic dislocation; it lasted about five years. John Tyler had become President of the United States in 1841, upon the death of William Henry Harrison; John Tyler would hold office until 1845.

Col. Francis Dana Newcomb

Col. Francis Dana Newcomb (1802-1872) was William A. Thomson's father-in-law. Col. Newcomb's father was Judge Richard English Newcomb (1770-1849) and his mother was Phoebe (Cushman) Newcomb (1771-1802). Col. Newcomb's stepmother was Mary (Warren) Newcomb (1771-1826), daughter of Dr. Joseph Warren (1741-1775) of Bunker Hill. Col. Newcomb graduated from West Point in the Class of 1824, and later served as Surveyor General of Louisiana (a Federal position). When I was a boy, my mother told me that Col. Newcomb was an illustrious ancestor, of whom I should be proud. My later research turned up information my mother never told me: he misappropriated large amounts of government money, destroyed substantial evidence, was arrested and charged, broke out of jail, and fled to Cuba. American extradition efforts were unsuccessful. While in Cuba, his business interests included slave dealing. He harbored the fugitive Major Thomas Turner, commandant of the infamous Libby Prison in Richmond, where Union prisoners were kept in horrendous conditions. After Col. Newcomb died in Cuba, his remains were buried in Baton Rouge. I donated Col. Newcomb's Havana diary to the American Antiquarian Society.

Lavinia Day (Newcomb) Thomson

Lavinia Day (Newcomb) Thomson (1828-1882) was William A. Thomson's wife. They married in 1848 in Greenfield, Massachusetts. The marriage took place after Lavinia's father Col. Francis D. Newcomb had been the subject of a Federal criminal prosecution and had fled to Cuba; this may have impaired her ability to find a respectable American-born husband, but the Scottish-born William A. Thomson was pleased to marry her, and they lived happily ever after, "till death do us part." Lavinia Day (Newcomb) Thomson had four lines of descent from Mayflower passengers: two from William Bradford, one from Isaac Allerton, and one from Richard Warren. She was also related to the Roeblings (as in the Brooklyn Bridge). She was buried near her husband at Saint Mark's Anglican Church.

T. Kennard Thomson

T. Kennard Thomson (1864-1952) was William A. Thomson's son. He lived in Yonkers, New York. He conducted a civil engineering practice based in New York City, primarily involving bridge design and construction. He achieved high visibility when he recommended extending Manhattan Island about a mile into New York Harbor. I donated the T. Kennard Thomson papers to Columbia University in the City of New York.

The first page of the typescript version of William A. Thomson's manuscript was on the civil engineering firm letterhead of T. Kennard Thomson. Thus, the typescript version was probably typed by T. Kennard Thomson or someone on his staff.

Further Information

Further information about William A. Thomson can be found in the Dictionary of Canadian Biography, which is available online. William A. Thomson's only prior published work is An Essay on Production, Money, and Government (1863), which is available from at least two print-on-demand services. Information about his economic theories can be found in Craufurd D.W. Goodwin, "A Forgotten Forerunner of Social Credit: William Alexander Thomson," Journal of Canadian Studies (Peterborough, Ontario), Volume 4, Issue 2 (May 1969), pages 41-45. Information about his railroad activities can be found in Robert D. Tennant Jr., Canada Southern Country (Erin, Ontario: The Boston Mills Press, 1991).

Timeline of Significant Events

Birth of William A. Thomson in Stranraer, Scotland	1816
Emigration of William A. Thomson from Scotland	1834
Travels of William A. Thomson	1842-1844
Discharge of Francis D. Newcomb from Federal service	1845
Federal criminal proceedings against Francis D. Newcomb	1846
Escape of Francis D. Newcomb from jail; flight to Cuba	1847
Marriage of William A. Thomson and Lavinia D. Newcomb	1848
Publication of An Essay on Production, Money, and Government	1863
Election of William A. Thomson to Canadian Parliament	1872
Death of William A. Thomson at Queenston, Ontario	1878

Denominational Affiliation of William A. Thomson

William A. Thomson described himself in Chapter 2 of the typescript as a Unitarian. The records of Trinity Episcopal Church in Buffalo record the baptism of my great-grandmother Mary Eleanor Thomson, daughter of William Alexander and Lavinia Day Thomson, on June 29, 1854; thus, he may have become an Episcopalian by that time. His Ontario death certificate gave his denominational affiliation as Church of England (which is the same religion as the Episcopal Church). He was buried at St. Mark's Anglican Church in Niagara-on-the Lake, Ontario (again, the same religion as the Episcopal Church).

Appendices

At the end of this book are two appendices, from documents left in my mother's estate.

Appendix A is the text of a letter from William A. Thomson to his constituents dated November 10, 1873, which was about a year after he was elected to the Canadian Parliament. The letter was printed on one side of a letter-size sheet of paper. The letter contains much of intellectual substance; this can be contrasted with the social media sound bites of many politicians circa 2020, in which the intellectual content is nil.

Appendix B is the text of a memorial booklet printed shortly after William A. Thomson's death on October 1, 1878. It consists of twelve black-bordered pages, six inches by four inches.

INTRODUCTION[1]

A trip from Buffalo to New York, Hartford, Philadelphia, Baltimore, and Washington, then to Europe and return, by WILLIAM ALEXANDER THOMSON, who was born in Stranraer, Wigtownshire, Scotland, November 7th, 1816; came to America in a sailing vessel in 1834, and established a wholesale hardware business in Buffalo.

He was married in 1848 to Lavinia Day Newcomb, who was born in Florida of New England parents. Her father, Col. Francis Dana Newcomb, was a graduate of West Point.

William Alexander Thomson lived in Buffalo until 1850, when he moved to Fort Erie, Ontario, for some fourteen years, then back to Buffalo for three or four years, and finally to "Glencairn," near Queenston, in 1867, where he lived until his death in 1878.

He originated and built and managed the Erie and Niagara Railway, and then the Canada Southern - both now parts of the Michigan

Central – and was a member of the Dominion Parliament, representing the County of Welland, from 1872 to 1878.

CHAPTER 1

American Eastern Seaboard

O n January 17, 1842, I left Buffalo for a tour through the Eastern States, embracing a visit to New York, Philadelphia, Washington, and Baltimore, and as the intent was to gain information of a general nature I may fill this manuscript with trash and useful knowledge in such glorious confusion that I may ultimately entitle it the "New Curiosity Shop."

My fellow travelers from Buffalo to Albany were capital company. A broken-down speculator, a railroad engineer, and a real bull of loco-focoism,[2] and a lawyer to boot. Our speculator friend had gained wisdom by hard experience and said little, but the gentlemanly engineer of the great road that is to connect the Atlantic and Lake Erie by an unbroken line – elated with the vivacity of a locomotive on the glorious results of their enterprise, which would shower the immense products of the West into New York at all seasons, while civilization and intelligence would fly on the wings of steam to the farthermost corners of the Far West. My big bellied locofoco thought locomotives great humbug, public improvements to be ruin and banks the curse of mankind, railroad servants to be great rascals and taverns as imposing on the public. My friends were both wrong, the engineer in imagining impossible results and the loco on his desire to have the world stand still and the good old days of mush and milk and sauerkraut back again. Their amusing banter aside – railroads are doing wonders in this country, and although it is doubtful that the Erie and New York Railroads will ever pay the builders yet, it must do a vast amount of business and enrich the fertile country through which it runs. When this road is completed, there will be avenues of communication with Buffalo and the East sufficient to carry all the merchandise and passengers for a hundred years to come. Although I do not agree with my locofoco friend on railroads, we fully concur in exposing the Bank of the State of New York and those of every state south and west of it as the nest of infamous rascals, and who under the cloak of a bank charter, are robbing the community, unhinging and demoralizing society, and producing a state of anarchy and confusion, influence that a quarter of a century will scarcely clear away. It seems that the influence of a bank will deprive the most upright of all honesty if he enters the service. My own observations tell me that while the officers of a bank are robbing the institution for their own etc., they issue forth by example and conversation the seeds of dishonesty, extravagance, and ruin on the youthful merchants of this luxuriant land, who all have to live and learn, as few have patience to learn before they begin to learn. This country is now in an awful state, the prostration of confidence, morals, and mental energy, is followed by absolute want by thousands who have heretofore lived in sumptuous elegance. When friend Jonathan abuses England for her working poor, he ought to look nearer home and find the thousands of broken-down merchants, lawyers, speculators etc., who have not actually the wherewithal to buy a barrel of flour for their family, and the tens of thousands whose only means of obtaining the necessaries of life is by polite swindling; and just as sure as a pauper is to be found in England, so sure is the present allusion to this country's poverty true. Glorious land, the Most High, in His wisdom surely never created such beauty, such wealth and such a clime for the habitation of knavery. Corruption and all the depravity of poor fallen Man. No! No! Though now you wallow in the mire and stink from the depravities of your people, yet the blood of the Red Man and the depravity of the White will mingle in the forgetfulness of the past and the small band of honest and the just that still are to be found will yet come forth in the strength of uprightness and truth and renovate your soiled reputation.

In manufacture I am more at home than in moralizing – let us make a visit to Henry Burden, my clever countryman who by his invention in machinery has enriched the country of his adoption and made his own fortune.[3] Among the most important of the improvements of Mr. Burden is the puddle machine, by which he obviates the use of the trip-hammer in making bar iron. This improvement enables him to make twenty tons in the same time as they formerly made two. His machine for making a wrought spike is a wonderful thing. His new mode of making a horse shoe completely by machinery is also a valuable invention, and to cap all, he has the largest water wheel in the country. He makes nails, spikes, horse shoes, and bar iron, and by way of change sometimes builds a steamboat to skim the Hudson on a new principle.

New York is a city full of excitable and active men, and I fear the lazy and extravagant at the same time. Everything denotes great immorality and want of principle, and yet it is the chief mart of the country, giving an example for good or for evil all around.

Philadelphia, although not so elegantly built as New York, and with narrower streets, is still a most beautiful city – its marble doors, windows, and steps improve and enrich the appearance. The business is much divided, and a great number of merchants in proportion to the trade. Several articles of hardware are made cheaper than in England, such as glass, straw-knives, spades, and shovels. Among the greatest ornaments may be classed the water works and twin bridge.[4] The water is forced up on a hill, where it is filtered and then supplies the whole city. Railroads enter the city from many sections of the country. To a European, the city would appear better than New York. It has a solid appearance of somber wealth. The country of New Jersey between New York and Philadelphia is flat, tame, and miserable. The ladies, larger and better made than in any other city in America, are likewise good-looking.

Baltimore is a compact city of two and three story brick houses, few elegant mansions but many comfortable ones. The bay is beautiful, and the sail down the river to the ocean must be delightful, some 200 miles. This city is celebrated for its beautiful women and from my own observations at private parties, I must say they are the most beautiful creatures I ever beheld, well made, handsome feet and hands, and very good housewives, I am told. Sweet expressions, good language, and well educated. The houses are furnished with a degree of elegance that the wealthiest noblemen in the world could not surpass, and in taste most beautiful. Silver is the same at dinner and tea and the rarest and most expensive wines are placed before the guest. Hospitable, kind, and generous, good people, you have my continual prayer for your happiness and prosperity.

Washington, or rather the Capitol, for that is the chief if not the only object. The city consists of a few thousand third rate houses without order or embellishment. The grounds around the Capitol (some 25 acres) are well laid out and the walks excellent. The Capitol is a very large building, built of sandstone and painted white all over, which gives it the appearance of marble. The interior is occupied in every corner, and with the room of the Representatives one cannot but be pleased. Its pillars of beautiful agate are in themselves a wonder. The Library is well kept and a good room. The Hall of Paintings and Sculpture is a circular room lighted from above and shows the paintings to advantage. The Washington statue in the center has just been put up and does not please the Americans, and yet in my humble taste it is good.[5] The painting of Washington giving up his commission is excellent.[6] The Capture of Burgoyne is also very good[7] and Pocahontas' Baptism is very showy.[8] I consider the Capitol an object worth a long journey to examine. The ladies look small and pretty here, but not beautiful. My chance of judging, however, has been imperfect. I must not omit to say the Senate Chamber and Hall of the Supreme Court are both beautiful. The President's house, so-so. The country around is indifferent. I must not omit the Patent Office Gallery - the models not half so numerous as I expected, and three fourths of what I saw I considered abortions. The models are not well arranged, but some day it will become a very interesting place for the visitor.

The whole country from New York to Washington looks indifferent: broken-down fences, clumsy carts, mules, and poor houses present to the eye of the traveler. And the slaves are perfect representations of slavery in its worst form. I can but doubt the advantage of liberty to such a race. For what is liberty unappreciated or unenjoyed, but a fantasy which one dreams of but cannot unearth. From every source my information on this subject inclines me to believe, that happy is the negro who is a slave, in comparison with the free black. The negro of strong natural ability can always become free – then why trouble the state about the remainder who are as slaves well provided for, while as free they would starve?

Advantages of Buffalo as a place of purchase of produce for English account:

First – The quality could be more depended on, the barrels in better order, and twenty-five cents generally saved in price as compared with the New York market.

Second – The onerous charges of New York would be saved, as the flour could be sent to the ship at New York direct, and while an advantage exists in favor of Buffalo to the English house, the commission would be a good one for the buyer.

Bridgeport, Connecticut, is a pretty place, about 2,000 inhabitants – the manufactures are saddles and harnesses only. There is considerable wealth and no bustle.

Birmingham or Derby[9] is eleven miles from Bridgeport, and a place of manufacture - tacks, brass, spanables, pins, woodwork, finished axles, auger (barrels), G.S. spoons and G.S. combs, rolling copper, etc.

New Haven is a beautiful place, and may be considered the best town in Connecticut. Around are several manufactories, such as Blake Brothers (castors, locks, faucets, blind-fasteners, carriage springs, etc.).[10]

The buildings of Yale College are large and capacious, and evidently the college is flourishing. Trumbull's Gallery of Paintings is attached to the college and is quite interesting.[11] The best collection of minerals in the state is also to be seen here.

The surrounding country is very fine - bluff and undulating country is continually before the eye. The city is so very quiet, indeed strikingly so, you might fancy yourself in a splendid cemetery instead of a living city, and take every splendid mansion for a tomb.

Rev. Mr. Nichols - introduced to him by letter from Mr. Shelts and found him very intelligent and polite - his opinion of his own countrymen is capital - just my own. He gave me a letter to Jacob L. Clarke,[12] Minister, Waterbury.

Hartford, 22nd. The busiest city in Connecticut, well situated on the banks of the Connecticut River and doing the chief business of the state, is well built and full of large churches. I am not in mood for the descriptive at present; I will therefore leave it till my next visit.

I will remember it for Mr. Bolles's politeness and my business victory over Mr. David C. Collins,[13] who found his match for once.

23rd. The men in many cases are good looking. The ladies are small, tolerable good looks, plain dressers, wear hoods, and rather pale faced.

I have been to Monte Video, the highest mountain in the state, from which you see all Connecticut.[14] The panorama of mountain and valley, torrent, stream, and meandering river, the mountains covered with hoary rocks and stunted forest. The valley beautifully adorned with its hundred cities and villages; the sober virtue of the people being expressed by the many church steeples standing out in bold relief for the eye, from this distant point. Truly this is a lovely state – true, the land is niggardly and barren – but what of that? See the glorious beauty around you and enjoy the scene, for know, admiring gazer, that every house you see contains contented industry; freedom's banners protect them and the human mind is expanding around you to the full extent allowed by our gracious and bountiful God.

Connecticut is a regular manufacturing state; every village has its water-power and factories – the population is about 300,000. As a body, I consider the manufacturers respectably intelligent, but generally not so much versed in mankind as I expected to find them.

The women of this state appear generally thin, sickly looking creatures – neither figure, face, or expression.

While I like the people for their industrious habits, and the state for its wild grandeur, I see nothing else to admire. The people live very poor. I took a pot-luck dinner with the most refined manufacturer in the state, and a piece of corned beef and a potato, with a little pie, constituted the meal.

In every attempt to effect a business arrangement, I have succeeded in this state; therefore while I express my opinions of men and the state in general, I have a lively feeling of friendship for my confiding correspondents – February 26, 1842.

CHAPTER 2

Sailing Ship to Great Britain

The following notes are not "for general circulation," nor are they intended for the entertainment of any beyond a few intimate friends. Particularly, as I intend to take little pains in either composition or arrangement, and have no idea even of what I mean to write about.

New York – November 25, 1843 - This day we sail for the Old World, in the good ship Roscius – Captain Collins – both the best of their kind.[15] Getting on board the ship with the aid of a small steamer, everything appearing in great confusion, we made for sea; and although no band of music cheered us away, we had the merry "Yo Heave Ho" of the sailors. Soon our good vessel was covered with canvas, and she bent steadily to the work before her, that of carrying her freight and passengers to a distant clime. There is something in beholding the railroad locomotive start its journey, snorting and pulling its immense burden with the velocity of a bird through the air. It is a striking evidence of Man's gigantic intellect bestowed upon him by the Creator for great purposes. Still in majestic grandeur, a ship under her spread of canvas bounding and leaping over the ocean waves is incomparable; a noble ship, perfect in her proportions (as the most lovely woman) obedient to her helm, now kissing the gentle ripple as she parts the waves most affectionately, anon dashing through the raging sea, shaking her sides with very anger at the obstinacy of the elements which dare her advance – then flying before the mountain wave nearly as fast as the wave itself, and finally moving into her destined port gray with toil, yet as firm and saucy as ever, she embodies the beautiful, majestic, and noble as perfectly as aught else in Creation. On shore I have thought of the danger of crossing the ocean, but I have ever found that with my foot on the quarter deck of a proper and noble ship, I luxuriated in the idea of braving danger with such a friend, and found that fear was left behind. Next to lovely, gentle, and affectionate women, there is naught more worthy of admiration than a brave and weather-beaten ship. I am now on board as fine a vessel with a noble Commander as ever adorned the fickle deep.

My fellow passengers count a dozen. So far, I see nothing about them worth note – all so-so sort of people, English, American, Irish, and Scotch. As I am not likely to find much of the truly delightful about them, I will not scandalize my book by jotting the unpleasant or tame good-nature, which I may find in them.

26 November – 'Tis Sunday. God's gift to poor hard-working man, for the rest of his body and purification of his mind; the day is fit for the occasion, brightened by a generous sun and perfumed by a gentle breeze from the south. Sunday, and at sea. Great God, I thank Thee for all Thou hast ever done for Thy undeserving creature, and thank Thee for giving me the opportunity of quiet Sunday at sea, to judge myself and collect my wayward and sinful thoughts. For naught am I more grateful for the godlike kindness affection and favor of my dear friends in the United States - the warm and loving affection of American women, although hid behind a cold exterior, to those who know how to find it, will prove as cheering and confiding as the

kindness or affection of any other clime – God bless them one and all. Woman is the best part of Creation everywhere. Among the men of America, too, I have found much and great kindness and some friends. And the pleasure with which I look forward to meeting my friends in Auld Scotia, will be nearly equaled in reapproaching my new home.

Vain – restless – ambitious – Man, why fly from east to west, north to south; why not be content with the land of your birth, the home of your father, and the friend of your childhood – do you ever meet such contentment and enjoyment again? Are you ever repaid for what you throw away, alas? No – and when wearied with strife and the turmoil of ambition's path, you return to the home and grave of your forefathers, what do you find? (O most just though severe!) That the firm tyrant has sent all to their long homes, your fireside, where you used to gambol and laugh for very joy, desolate – and most true of all, your own feelings and affections so seared and destroyed, that enjoyment in new sources is denied to you – and you too must go down to the grave, perhaps unhonored, unwept, and unknown.

> Does the stork intent on rest,
> On the billow build her nest?
> No – No!
> Man alone intent to stray
> Ever errs in Wisdom's way.
> To lay up wealth in other lands
> He sails the sea and plows the land.[16]

Wednesday, November 29 – Since Sunday we have had a strong wind and favorable; sea sickness has been fashionable, and eating and drinking vulgar for the time. The poor fellows begin to show themselves or their ghosts, for they are only the shadows of their former selves, and the way we quiz them is to them intolerable. (I was sick for about half an hour and kept it secret.)

Some very warm discussion has been going on, in which without knowing why, I find I have been taking a leading part. For I am sure

I never would have entered the field on such a subject, voluntarily or purposely.

The senior passenger is an Englishmen, who has been making a tour of the United States, with his daughter. He is a Socialist, a Unitarian, a disbeliever in the Bible, a doubter of a hereafter, or punishment hereafter, a teetotaler, and a radical. Now I am a Unitarian, believe in the sacred character of the Bible, I indulge in matters of the table such as wine etc., and an out-and-out Tory. He delivered a sermon on Sunday evening, touching most of the above doctrines; after he had finished I took the liberty of questioning part of his doctrine, which involved an argument which continued upwards of six hours. He had the Captain and a Bostonian on his side, both loquacious; I had the rest of the passengers on my side, but I suppose they despised his principles so much that they declined entering the field of argument, which left me in a troublesome position.

Thursday, November 30, 1843. A gale cut short my scribbling yesterday, and it has been blowing tremendously ever since. We fly rather than sail and the waves are very large. A fair wind ever since we left New York and already (fifth day) one third of our voyage is completed. About twelve o'clock last night, after the moon had set I was on deck, the night was dark, the ship at a speed of twelve miles per hour, as she ploughed her way casting the foamy wave aside, on each side it became brilliant with golden luster, producing the peculiar phenomenon of water on fire, illuminating the darkness of the threatening ocean on every side, appearing like a Lady's Robe of purest white, studded deeply with jewels and gold rivaling each other in dazzling luster.[17]

It had become fashionable to treat matters of serious import lightly, but it strikes me more forcibly now than on any former voyage, that a voyage across the Atlantic is an event of serious reflection to a landsman, and he had better be dispensed with, when not absolutely necessary. I observe among our passengers, that those who are on their first voyage are the lightest hearted and appreciate least the serious risk of a winter trip across the stormy deep - while older travelers deeply enter into the thought of the prospect of danger; at the same time seeing and enjoying the wonder and grandeur of the mighty deep, which the young traveler overlooks, burying himself in his cabin most of the time.

Monday, December 4. To record the jokes and causes of merriment which help to drive away the dullness of the voyage, is useless; the joke would be as the body without the soul, in as much as the spirit of the joke dies with the occasion and would not be applicable at a different time and place. We spend one day pretty much as the preceding: reading, talking, and quizzing, and sometimes cards and toddy in the evening. On the 30th of Nov. I stated we had a heavy gale. Since then we have experienced a fearful hurricane.[18] This morning is pleasant, a fair and fine breeze and heavy sea, but yesterday and the day previous it blew as if it would blow its last. We scudded under the bare poles carrying only one little fore-sail to steady the ship. The waves were immense, and to venture a speculation on their height: I think when the ship was in the hollow or trough of the sea, she was, as it were, running into a breast work of water 50 feet above her. It was truly grand to witness the efforts of the noble ship as she overcame each succeeding difficulty. Now the sea threatening to overwhelm her, anon on the top of the highest wave, again plunging into the valley of water, to escape from which she had to contend with a new enemy, perhaps stronger than the one she had just escaped. By and by as if weakened by her constant combat, she is driven aside staggered and nearly overwhelmed by her enemy, but again she rallies to the conflict and victory crowns her endeavors, for the salvations of herself, passengers, and crew. Today she looks (with all her sail spread to the breeze) as saucy and placid as if she had already forgot the terrible hurricane of yesterday and the previous day. Our worthy Captain tells us that he had seldom witnessed the like in any previous voyage. Many of our passengers were alarmed, especially those who had not been at sea before, although they were the most cocksure in decent weather. To those aware of the properties of a good ship well commanded, there is a confidence inspired during a storm which annihilates fear, and such, with pride in their eye, glory in the struggle of the good ship, and feel that she and they are one. It is decent weather that the brave men weigh the danger of crossing the mighty deep, and fears; in the storm and hurricane, when it comes, no fear fills his mind. When smooth weather returns, he is grateful to Providence of the safety for all. How different with the weak and cowardly mind – in smooth water, braggadocious – in a storm, cowards all!

A fair wind still favors us as it has, ever since we left New York.

Wednesday, December 6. We are getting forward toward our port of destination gradually yet surely. The winds for the past two days have been fickle; now a steady and strong breeze drives us on.

We have seen neither ship nor fish since we left New York, and for any evidence to the contrary, we have the ocean to ourselves. We are out eleven days, and the steam ship from Boston is out six days today. It is a matter of much speculation and gambling among us, whether we are to arrive before or after the steamer. If present winds continue we will beat her.

Riddle made by the Archbishop of Canterbury.

1
I sit here on a rock; while I am raising the wind.
But when the storm's over, I am gentle and kind.
The Kings of the Earth lie down at my nod.
And tread in the dust, that I have just trod.
Though oft seen in the world, I'm known to but few.
The Gentiles detest me, I'm pork to the Jew.

2
I never have spent but one night in the dark.
And that was with Noah alone in the Ark.
I weigh but three pounds but I measure a mile.
And when you have guessed me, I'll say with a smile,

My first and my last are the best of our Isle.[19]

Saturday, December 9. Since Wednesday we have been running through the water at a great speed, not less than 250 miles per day, and if the wind holds good for 48 hours longer, we will be in Liverpool (a passage of 15 ½ days.)

The porpoises and gulls keep us company now, and break the dreariness of the ocean, which we have had so much to ourselves; for a winter passage it has been rapid and on the whole pleasant; true, we have had heavy gales and one awful storm, but smooth water and a fair wind soon makes danger past forgotten. The constant rolling of the vessel, which makes it impossible to walk straight, sit, or lay steadily, irritates the nerves, and makes a painful feature in a sea voyage. But this and all else are forced from the memory, as we approach land and know that our stay is limited.

Monday, December 11, 1843. The pilot on board, the ocean crossed, our voyage at an end, and terra firma under our eye - Hurra! Hurra! For Old England's good hearts, strong friends, and enemies of oppression. Your isles surrounded by mist look gloomy enough, but that only tends to enhance the honest welcome you give your friend.

A romping, laughing, and merry day this has been, passengers crazy, seeing who could see farthest, tell the biggest story, make the kindest speeches, and offer the nicest welcome to each other's place of abode. Boisterous and threatening ocean, you are a rough chiel[20] to cope with, but fighting you makes many kind friends, and really, now I have again shaken your shaggy mane without your punishing me, I leave you in good feeling, and will again venture to play with you in recrossing to my Western home, by and by. Meantime I am in Old England, my own, my native land. God bless her.

On the 12th the passengers of the Roscius gave Captain Collins a dinner at the "Star and Garter," as an expression of their perfect satisfaction with him as a gentleman and a sailor. My brother passengers did me the honor of placing me in the Chair on the occasion. The thing went off well and now we are all scattered, never to meet again. Not a quarrel occurred among us and harmony, joviality, and mirth continued to the last minute.

December 14. On board the steam boat <u>Athlone</u>, from Liverpool to Belfast.

CHAPTER 3

Belfast and Donaghadee

Liverpool is a well-built town, its buildings for public purposes and churches are very fine, and the shops are equal, indeed superior to Broadway. The horses and carts of immense size are wonders to look at. I must cease to write, for strange to say, I grow sea sick here, although I crossed the Atlantic a few days ago without suffering – confound this quivering, shaking, pitching boat - I wish I were at Belfast. More of Liverpool by and by.

Belfast, Ireland, December 15, 1843. Such a night as I passed on the steam boat, from Liverpool to this place, where I arrived this morning, I do not wish to pass again. Very sea sick, a storm the whole night – when we reached this bay we were too late for the tide and had to anchor three miles below the city, from thence conveyed in small row boats to town. It was still blowing, with a heavy swell for such sized boats; however, in we bundled bag and baggage, up went the little sail, and away we flew. In a short time we were completely drenched, and the wind proving unfavorable, down went the sail, and the men took to their oars, pulling right in the teeth of the wind and sea. The boat was quarter full of water, the baggage was half afloat, and to crown my part of this delightful predicament, away went my hat overboard. The boat was drifted back and my hat caught, but full of water and too wet to put on. Paddy, with his usual politeness, offered me his glazed Carter, but it looked so greasy and suspicious inside, that I refused it; he then offered me a large shawl wrapper which he had round his neck, which I accepted, and made my entry into this city with a shawl round my head.

The experience which I gained when a boy, regarding sailing boats, and the risks I then undertook from sheer love of excitement, enabled me to form an estimate of the danger we ran in going to Belfast from the steamer, and I am now sure, that the journey and voyage from Buffalo to Liverpool was less hazardous for life and less destructive to clothes, than the miserable landing at this place. I meditated reaching this city in time for the morning coach to Donaghadee, where I would have got today's steamer to Galloway, but our long voyage made our arrival some hours too late, and I have therefore devoted this day to visiting the different parts of this city.

Belfast is known as an active mercantile city, being the principal city of export and import for the North of Ireland.[21] Its exports are provisions, linens, and cotton goods, principally. The bay is good but the great rise and fall of the tide is a great obstacle to its shipping interests. There are half a dozen humdrum streets and respectable houses on each side of them. The public buildings are good and commodious, but not particular for beauty. Irish masons must be miserable, for I do not see a house built well. They put too much lime between the bricks and point them shockingly; this, added to the bad quality and color of the brick, makes the finest houses look shabby. Excepting the principal streets, the others are very narrow, paved with small stones, sidewalks and all – the sidewalks three feet wide and the houses two stories high, the roof not over fourteen feet from the ground and the roofs very steep. The face of these small streets, which constitutes three fourths of the town, are occupied as shops for groceries, meat, and small taverns; small lanes pass from these streets into courts behind, which are surrounded by dwelling houses, similar to the ones facing the street. They all look dirty and evidently unused to much scrubbing. The men look as if they washed and shaved twice a week, and the boys once a week. The women and girls look as if they washed their faces every day; they all keep their necks covered, perhaps to hide dirt.

The shops in the principal streets are very good, but nothing remarkable about them. The fashionable streets are crowded with men of business and ladies, the latter evidently there for purpose of business only, for they walk as fast as the men. The men look like good livers – bluff faces, plain and respectable in their appearance and gait. The gentlemen dress well and cheap – the men in lower scale are clean and free from rags in their outward clothes, modest and respectful in their look and manner, evidently intent on their own affairs. I have been in all sorts of corners on the piers, through the lanes, in public places and streets all day without seeing a drunk man or woman, and only had two demands for charity.

I have never seen any city where the women, high and low, look so pretty as in this. In Liverpool I was struck with want of general beauty, here ugliness is the exception. The ladies are plain and heavily dressed on the streets, still their carriage is commanding and graceful, their features regular, rosy, and white; eyes dark – altogether a fine style of beauty – ankles a little too stout and feet pretty good. In walking they do not swing their haunches and shuffle their feet as my American friends do, but still they have a side roll which begins at their shoulders, descends to the foot and lifts it clean off the ground to be placed in advance, then the counter roll sends the other foot ahead. This style of progression gives a saucy and careless appearance in their carriage, while it is free from coquetry, while the American ladies' mode of walking is quite coquettish (but what am I about, criticizing my dear little friends in America!).

The women of middle class are pretty, of clear complexions and I noticed very many of them had clean white woolen stockings, and well brushed shoes on, all busily engaged in some occupation, some shopping, some keeping shops, working at their windows, etc. The ladies in their dress, cover close up to their chin, the middle and lower class wear low dresses, with a thick shawl up to their neck, which is pinned toward their waist, leaving a small part of their breast bare, and as they have all heavy chests, it gives them the appearance of being chicken-breasted, although I do not suppose it is so.

Belfast situated as it is, at the head of a large bay, itself a compact town, has around it as beautiful scenery as you could wish to behold. On two sides fine hills and mountains cultivated to the very top, studded with many elegant country seats, which with the hedges, plantations, farm houses, etc., make a pretty "tout ensemble." Although winter, yet my sense of hearing was charmed with the carol of a thousand birds, in some of the squares of the town where there were trees to shelter them. Mr. Hannay, an extensive merchant in this town, called upon me and took me to his house to pass the evening. My surprise was great when I found in his wife and her sister whom I met, two young Galloway girls, who knew me and all about me. They were truly beautiful and Hannay had transplanted one of them to the Green Isle for life. But after all Belfast is more Scotch than Irish. Hannay is of Scotch descent and distantly related to me. They all speak with more of the Scotch than Irish accent. From my young Galloway friends I got all the news of Stranraer and Wigtownshire, spent an agreeable evening and the following morning entered an Irish car for Donaghadee. The country between the two places is good for crops, and tolerably farmed, but not equal to Scotch fencing and farming. I find as regards Scotch farming that since my last visit to Scotland, they have extensively drained the wet farming lands, with what is called tile draining – making the drains about 24 feet apart and placing the tile about two feet deep. These tiles are made of clay and burned like brick, about twelve inches in length and eight inches wide with corresponding concave, so that one laid in the bottom of the drain and another on the top thereof make a complete tube. After this is laid it is covered with earth, and the drainage from the land enters this tube at the sides and ends of each twelve inch section, and whatever sand enters with the water is by the evenness and force of the channel carried away with the water; whereas in stone drainage the sand becomes baked with the stones and ultimately chokes the passage of the water, rendering such a drain useless. Fencing has also been attended to, and everything in agricultural Scotland looks like growing intelligence and comfort beyond what I expected to find.

But to return to my trip from Belfast to Donaghadee. On my arrival at the latter place after a two hours' ride, I was much surprised to find my recollections clear and strong on some incidents of my life which occurred when I was only three years old. At the period my parents sojourned in Donaghadee for some time, and while there I had for a playmate a little girl of my own age, with whom I went one day on the beach while the tide was out, and took our seat on a very large stone or rather small rock on which grew dulce,[22] which we proceeded to gather and eat. While thus employed the tide had been rising and before we discovered, a sheet of water opposed our return to shore, and by and by the rock on which we sat would be covered and our lives lost, for two such children could not have made themselves heard on shore, which was at full tide some hundred yards from the rock on which we sat. Prompt action was necessary under such circumstances, although the sheet of water now between us and the shore was broad, yet it was not too deep for me to wade. Although of the same age, I was stronger and larger than my little companion, and to this moment I often smile at the natural gallantry which impelled me to take my little friend on my shoulder and plunge sturdily through the advancing tide for the shore, which advanced nearly as fast as I did. I well recollect the exhaustion which overpowered me when the trial was over and the little thing kissing me and refusing to leave me. We finally reached my home, our clothes were changed, and to end the story, I smuggled a cloak of my mother's which we took to the drawing room least used, we wrapped ourselves in it, and after a display of childish affection, enveloped head and feet in the cloak and stretched on the carpet as we went to sleep in each other's arms. As soon as I saw Donaghadee the whole thing flashed in my memory, I saw the rock on which we sat, but could not recognize the house in which we lived. I had only five minutes to stay as the steam-boat waited for us, but in that time I found a person who told me all about my little playmate, now a young lady of eight and twenty and unmarried. I sent my love to her on a card, although much tempted to wait a day and see her - and soon the boat carried me and my wishes toward the Scottish shore.

CHAPTER 4

Stranraer and Ayr

As the little boat approached the ironbound coast of Scotland, the dreams of boyhood began to float before my imagination, but the joyousness of that era had left me. I still enjoy and am happy, but no longer that wild enthusiastic feeling of delight in revisiting old spots and friends. However I find myself in Scotia once more, and am glad that it is so. Portpatrick, where I landed, to Stranraer is eight miles; this distance I performed on the outside of the coach; every field, fence, stream, morass, heather, hill, and house we passed was familiar to me, and each had some incident connected with it, which I brought to memory as we proceeded. There, where myself and father and grandfathers were born, the old venerable house still standing, now occupied by strangers, no tie existing to recall me to the spot, and no old known face to welcome me. In Stranraer I find my friends diminished; time has done its work and the grave has received many sweet and kind friends, whom I had hoped to see again. Of those yet alive, a great proportion are on the verge of their departure to another world, and should another five years elapse before I revisit this country, there will be no inducement to take me to Galloway. My youngest friends are upwards of forty years in age, and most above sixty years of age. The place of those who departed is filled by strangers from other parts of Scotland, and Galloway is fast becoming to me a foreign land. The kindness of all is as great and unbounded as ever; each vie with the other, who can show me most attention. The women, God bless them, young and old, are not frightened by cold etiquette from being kind and attentive to me. It cost me much pain to run away from them with a sound heart, but I succeeded in conquering myself.

(gap in manuscript)

her large family and without anything except her little furniture, is sent away unpensioned and unaided. For the life of service and fidelity of her husband to the Stair family,[23] she is condemned to absolute want in her helpless widowhood. It makes me savage to imagine this miserly and cold hearted Lord (and his sycophantic factotum of a factor who should have pressed the matter to this new Lord's attention), refusing a paltry pension to the widow of a faithful follower, who has served three generations of the same family, while he has by his predecessor's death inherited 40,000 pounds per annum, from which he grudges 20 or 30 pounds per annum. Moral: if I ever live again in this country (which is extremely unlikely), I shall give my voice against the law of entail, which protects such brutes in station and wealth. The massacre of Glencoe was the act of a Stair;[24] the character of the men of Stair is evidently not much improved since.

This visit to Stranraer confirms my previous opinion that the situation of Stranraer and the scenery around is of a superior character in beauty, and that I question my ever having seen a more lovely spot. That the town is compact and somewhat dirty, is of no great consequence in itself. Its inhabitants of the old school, including the young branches of the old families, are very polished, high bred, and noble hearted people, whom I am more inclined to admire the more I see them. The great majority of them I will probably never see again. I cannot help observing that many families are in their last generation, having none to succeed them. This rises from natural causes not necessary to note.

Ayr, the town of Burns, is a beautiful place, indeed the whole ride from Stranraer to Glasgow is through a beautiful country. Although I stayed a short time at Ayr, I deem it best to avoid a description until I see more of it – the banks of the Doon, and so forth.

CHAPTER 5

Glasgow

Glasgow is vastly improved since my last visit. The grandeur and beauty of every street is beyond aught I have seen since last here. Its commerce is still growing, and around in every direction for miles above miles, you see hundreds of immense manufactories, producing luxuries for every corner of the globe.

Every house and street is built of freestone, which is polished, and being so easily cut, all the doors and windows of good houses are ornamented with carving. The buck shaped stone with which the streets are paved, make quiet and smooth thoroughfares. The want of sculpture is the only failing in the beauty of the architecture of this city. I notice a new style of window which I admire. With good glass, the effect of this new window is much better than the old twelve-pane up and down kind of sash and glass.

The chief point of difference between a Glasgow and an American city house is in the basement arrangements. In America the basement is often used partly as a dining room, here as a kitchen, laundry, cellar, coal house, servant's room, etc., to wit, see the basement ground plan of the friend's house I am now staying with. In the scullery there is a furnace which heats water and sends it up to the baths in the upper part of the house. By this division of rooms, the kitchen is devoted to cooking entirely. The washing room has its own furnace and boiler. The scullery heats bathing water and leaves the kitchen fire and range to be adapted peculiarly to cooking. On one side you find a stationary oven; on the other, a stationary kettle boiler for warm water. A roasting jack is placed to cook with a spit in front of the fire – a place for warming dishes; in short, everything is very complete. In the scullery, arrangement is made for washing dishes, with either cold or hot water; to get either, you only have to turn a cock in the very vessel in which you want to use this water.

Another difference - in America after you enter the front door, the stair to the second story commences at the threshold, and the room (drawing or dining, as the case may be) door is close to the front entrance; here, the stair begins about the middle of the house – and the entrance to the parlor is at the end farthest from the street entrance. I decided in favor of the Glasgow plan for two reasons: first, it ensures more warmth to the room, and second, the stair being so far back allows a hall door inside, between which and the outside door, hats and cloaks etc. can be placed.

The level of the halls above the street is three to four feet, which is ascended by wide steps.

A rage for paintings exists in Glasgow, but good taste is not the people's character in this department.

Oak panel painting has been the style of ceiling for dining rooms: flock or red walls and oak wainscot. It looks very fine but is getting out of fashion. Now they adopted a harmony of colors – say, at the cornice edge of ceiling and near the ground, yellow, azure blue, or other stripes or lines, running around the room, then the rest of walls one color and the ceiling some other color, according to taste of the owner or painter.

Gas is introduced to every house, and most use it in dining or drawing rooms, although it is considered vulgar by some.

Dining room furniture is all mahogany and chairs are very heavy, the bottom and back stuffed with hair and covered generally with crimson morocco.

The drawing rooms are often rosewood furniture, enveloped in chintz. The rooms look overfurnished, with sofas, ottomans, chairs, and old-fashioned card tables – from India or elsewhere.

Bedrooms the very essence of comfort, large covered arm chair, curtained bed, foot tub, set in mahogany, wash stand with every convenience, small library chairs covered with chintz, closet and baths attached and so on.

Servants, perfection itself. They seem to know their duty as well as their mistress, and perform it quietly and quickly.

With a Glasgow man his house is his home, his theater, his place of amusement, the school for his family, until they reach ten or twelve years – in short, the only place where he is to be found after five o'clock each day – hence their sumptuous comfort in furnishing their home.

Society is not a very refined character, the ladies have no influence, and every refinement withers before the all-powerful excitement of trade. The dinner table occupies from five to nine o'clock each day, and the drawing room presents weak attractions to the gentlemen, who prefer to sip the wine and talk business – instead of spending most of the evening in the drawing rooms. It is difficult to find a person who will converse on the advance of a science, travels, history, or aught else not applicable to everlasting trade.

A good story was told in my presence the other evening at a friend's house. My friend was giving a distinguished dinner party. During dinner we were moderately agreeable, and the ladies retired to the drawing room. Thinking the gentlemen stayed too long over their wine, I stole away to the ladies, whom I found telling traveling anecdotes. A lady most superbly dressed, large and good looking, began with a strong Glasgow accent to say – "That a certain doctor of divinity found himself in a railway car with only one lady for a companion. They became very loquacious and ultimately grew tired and fell asleep. Next morning the train had reached the stopping place of the learned doctor, who on leaving his traveling companion, wished her good-bye, saying, 'Madame, it will be a long time before you and I sleep together for a whole night again.'"

This lady, by the accumulated wealth of her husband, was tolerated in Glasgow society; and although a rich robe and jewels covered her body, it was not able to hide the vulgarity of her low mind, or she would not have insulted the delicacy of refined women with so ridiculous a story, of an equally vulgar divine.

Ladies only dress here for parties, and then with indifferent taste.

There are many elegant and refined families in the city, but I fear the majority are only moderately refined and enlightened. Gentlemen are very hospitable and ladies are very kind, and both manufactures and commerce are conducted on an extent and with a substantial splendor, which indicates great intellect and strong morality.

The late division of the established church has made a bad feeling in Scotch society. It has divided families, parted friends, and increased the influence of the clergy. I am not able to say whether the dissenters are right or not, but I hope all will settle down to peace and harmony again, and that the church will become stronger than ever in the minds and hearts of the Scotch people.[25]

The women of Scotland are completely excited on the church subject, and much under the influence of the clergy, a body whom I consider as dangerous advisers for women, from their limited knowledge of mankind and the world.

During this visit I have been much struck with the training and education of youth in Scotland. In play, in dressing, at meals, in short under every situation, the parent is constantly talking to the children, and inculcating honesty, truth, activity, politeness, and every other quality and virtue which elevates and adorns man. This constant state of moral training, added to a thorough education, will continue to elevate the Scotch, and rub off the unpleasant traits which have characterized the country, while in a poorer state.

The feeling is to elevate the schoolmaster to the social station of the minister and thereby obtain more highly gifted and better-bred men to fill the teacher's chair. This is no doubt proper and I think it will ultimately be the case. The great attention paid to improving education and increasing the mental power is surely fraught with great advancement to this country and people. It is a silly notion that this country has reached the zenith of its greatness and glory. It appears to me as if they were only beginning to develop the powers of that gigantic intellect, which as a people they naturally possess - and which, only half developed, has made themselves and country, what they are in fame, freedom, happiness, wealth, and power.

Although writing of Glasgow, I may here note, that I am in England and have been for some weeks, and that my reflections on Glasgow are from notes, tempered by what I have seen since. Having said this much, I will now say a few words on the poverty of Glasgow and England generally. Although I have not read a certain book, called The Glory and Shame of England,[26] yet I am told that the poverty and misery of this country is great and terrible, according to the observations of the author of said book.

In England and Scotland, when the population is dense, as in cities, there is necessarily a large body of poor and squalid people. But in times of moderate prosperity in trade, and the number is not great in proportion to the whole population - the law is such that none can starve. The "poor houses" are prepared to grant abundance of food and raiment to all who really deserve it, and this is done without compelling them to live in the "poor houses," and it thus follows that the paupers who pester you in the streets are neither numerous nor deserving. They are composed of two parties, one which is daily fed from the poor house, yet begs besides for profit, and the other class are petty swindlers, too lazy and depraved to submit to work for their living, and who find a pleasure in this Gypsy mode of gaining a livelihood. A house to live in is offered for them – food, raiment, and medical attendance, to provide which the wealthy population is heavily taxed and the tax paid with pleasure. Besides the aforementioned "poor house" and City Poor Houses, private individuals are constantly endowing houses for the same purpose. These facts place the pauperism of this country in a fair light, and are no serious charge against the character of the nation – for if we look into the causes of poverty and misery, and it will be found that misbehavior and guilt produce nearly all the poverty and ultimate distress – in time of prosperity the labor of every man is in demand, but laboring men are badly educated, and I may say, women too, for I speak of both. They think not of tomorrow, and instead of saving for bad times, they spend in foibles and follies what they make beyond the cost of their living – when the bad times arrive and their work is stopped for a few weeks – their minds weakened by previous excess - are fairly paralyzed by the check in their income, they have accustomed themselves so long to their beer and whiskey, that with the last sixpence they fly to it for comfort, finish by committing petty theft or habitual drunkards no longer fit for honest labor and paupers for life, accordingly. Again, accidents unfitting men afterwards for labor, sometimes make paupers. Unforeseen calamities (generally the result of weak and uncultivated minds) fall upon some, paralyze the mind and reduce to poverty those born in better circles of society. But to finish, the great mass of pauperism is the result of crime and ignorance; true, this is equally disgraceful or more so than pauperism, but it is the natural result of that state of society when money making is the chief and most powerful bent of the peoples' character. This is an evil passing away; science and learning are crushing with contempt this too great love of money, and I find all the better class of men devoting much of their time to curing the causes of poverty, by raising up the poor to a higher level through education, moral instruction, and affording constant employment to all.

This country by situation and through possessions in every clime has advantage over every other country.

This country, from the inventions and ingenuity of the past and present population, is far in advance of the rest of the world in manufacturing ability, in extent of capital, and in mercantile knowledge.

The country, sensibly alive to the advantage of education and science, already superior to any country in the number of highly and thoroughly cultivated minds which she possesses, and most abundantly blessed with natural energy of character, has more means of education and more ability from the situation of her population of extending it to all (to an extent that will ultimately, and before long, make every mind in the Kingdom of a superior and productive character) than any other country.

Therefore, I argue, that education now being applied to the poor, will elevate them above poverty. Extended and extending production in manufactures, in mining, aye and in farming (for science is making even farming here what I never knew it before – where the labor of one man was all that could be given to a patch of land, science makes it necessary to employ two, making the land feed more and pay more profit), offer a secure field for the educated poor to rise in, if they have superior ability by nature. If not, it offers a certain employment which their education will turn to good account – and vice, crime, and poverty will become less and less under the elevating influence of education and good example.

In Glasgow I noticed a growing taste for flowers, chemistry, and geology. The botanical garden belonging to the city is very fine and the collection in and out of the greenhouses large and rare.

The old and noble Cathedral of Glasgow, now styled by the John Knox man "High Church," is a very interesting structure - beside it there is a steep and high hill, divided from the cathedral by a deep ravine, which the people have selected for a necropolis or burying ground. I cannot agree with the worthy townsmen in their taste; it is bare, very steep, and incapable of adornment by shrubbery or trees - no green walks or shaded avenues - its only atmosphere the smoke from surrounding manufactories. If they had selected the Botanical Garden grounds for a burying ground, there would have been more taste, according to my notion. I have written thus much because I differ from all my friends in Glasgow on the subject.

Beside the cathedral there stands a unique cottage, in which Mary Stuart and Lord Darnley lived for some time.[27] It is now a small tavern called Lord Darnley's Tavern.

A little further down High Street there is a modern house having nothing particular about it, except that the windows vary in size and look ridiculous - upon mentioning it to a friend, he assured me as a fact, that the old fellow who built it, had bought some sash with glass in it at an auction very cheap, and actually built a four-story house to suit the window frames.

A new method of washing clothes has been discovered here, namely to put the dirty clothes in a tub, and pour cold water upon them, with which you put some bleaching powder. This is done in the evening - next morning the clothes should be turned around for a minute with a stick, then nothing has to be done but wrench them out in clean water - they become perfectly clean without soap, hot water, scrubbing, boiling, etc. I should call this a real improvement.

The club houses of Glasgow are on a style of great magnificence. Entrance fee twenty pounds and annual payment afterwards ten pounds, for which you become part owner of a mansion (a palace in fact) with a paid retinue of livery servants: superb cooks and a first-rate master of ceremonies.

All the principal papers and period periodicals are taken by the house. There is a reading room, smoking room, writing room, dining room, drawing room, and private conversation rooms, also a few chambers for country members. A stock of wine is kept in the cellar, and the choicest eatables in the pantry, and the only thing you have to pay for is any eating, drinking, or smoking you enjoy in the house. The furniture, house, and style, is more elegant or equal to the very finest private mansion in the city. And as one Black Ball prevents an election, the subscribers of each club are most agreeable and select. The laws which govern the club are strict, no conversation in the reading room; in short, a room for everything and everything is done in the proper place.

A splendid ball was about to be given by one of the clubs, to which I was invited but am sorry I had to decline, as it would have kept me too long in Glasgow.

CHAPTER 6

Loch Lomond and Edinburgh

Scotch railroads are fine affairs, built to last for ages, and on a style of grandeur really extravagant. The terminus of the Edinburgh Railway is covered by the finest iron self-supporting roof I ever saw, 200 feet wide without a single intermediate pillar, walls and roof entirely of iron. I timed the speed of this road for ten miles; it was exactly at the rate of 40 miles per hour.

I visited Loch Lomond, certainly the most beautiful romantic spot in Scotland. The beauty, silent yet deep, of the loch with its isles and precipitous coast. Hoary Ben Lomond towering up to heaven, its top hid in masses of fleeting clouds, leaving the imagination to portray its height beyond the cloudy way, and looking like the mighty giant protector of the placid and lovely loch below. In this neighborhood you have of course, the Leven, Balloch, etc., noted in song.

Copy of unpublished lines in the possession of Joshua Scholefield, M.P. for Birmingham:[28]

Nobody is missed.

The world is gay and fair to us, as now we journey on,

Yet still 'tis sad to think 'twill be the same when we are gone.

Some few, perchance may mourn for us, but soon the transient gloom

Like shadows of the summer cloud, shall leave our narrow tomb.

For men are like the waves that roll along the mighty deep.

That left their crest awhile and frown, and then are lulled to sleep.

While other billows swelling come, amid the foam and spray,

And as we view their burrowy tract, sink down, and where are they?

And ever thus the waves shall roll, like those but now gone past,

The offspring of the depths beneath, the children of the blast.

And ever thus shall men arise, and be like those that be.

And a man no more be missed on land, than a wave upon the sea.[29]

Edinburgh. This visit has strengthened my opinion that a more beautiful city cannot exist, the situation so lovely, picturesque, and grand, the tasteful arrangement of the streets, the superb architecture of the public buildings, the monuments, the Castle, the Palace, the antiquity of the old town, the rich historic story of the town in bygone centuries, and the happy pen of Walter Scott,[30] make the capital of Scotland one of the most interesting cities in the world.

The people look healthy, educated, and refined, bearing evidence of superior manners to any other town in Scotland. The railway to Glasgow, I timed the train at 40 miles an hour, which is beautiful speed.

CHAPTER 7

Chester and Liverpool

February 8. For a month past I have been in England, and during the whole time among the manufactories of the country, but have been so engrossed with business and scenes of interest in a business way, that my journalizing has been fairly overlooked. To now write up, all I have seen during the past month is more than I have diligence for at present, and sure of remembering all I saw. Now my business is ended. My usual good fortune has aided me in doing thoroughly all I wished to accomplish here, and I now feel in good courage for two months' exploration. We will begin where I now am, at Chester. A walled city, the wall in thorough preservation although built originally by the Romans. The length of the wall is one and three-quarter miles, and a beautiful flagged walk on its top, round the whole city. The streets are narrow and the houses are strangely constructed on street shops, above these shops again moved back so as to have a street on top of the first shops, over which second street the two and three story dwelling houses project so as to form a covered street, which continues from one end to another of each

street. Other streets have the second story projecting far over the first story, so as to cover the passer-by from rain.

The cathedral is a noble old building, decidedly the most interesting sight here. Its spacious aisles, elegant arches, marble floors, oak carvings, and fine toned organ, make it delightful for the visitor. I attended a service, which is performed every day. The musicians are boys and men with white gowns. The music of the voice and organ was quiet, solemn and soul stirring, no gaudiness about it, thorough church music. The priest read the prayers with a sweet and refined voice and accent; a fine mind highly cultivated for the service of God and His church. The immense aisles, very high roof, no seats, gorgeous windows, and sculptured walls add to the deep solemnity with which man's mind should be attuned when he approaches his God. Each time I enter such a building I am more and more impressed with the propriety of the ancient and gorgeous style being adapted to all churches. It can do no harm and is nearly certain to do much good. From thinking and cultivated man God deserves the utmost reverence, and our best taste in erecting houses to His worship, and the greatest care in procuring the best and holy for our priest, is surely what is due to Him who has given us the power to refine and improve ourselves.

The scenery from the walls of Chester is very fine: in the far distance you have the bleak mountains of Wales or Anglesey, between you have in your eye a beautifully cultivated country with its seats and hedges, around the city the River Dee flows, and away in a forest you can just see the tops of one of the finest mansions in England, the seat of the Marquis of Westminster.

The inhabitants of this town look more delicately formed than in the neighboring shires of Stafford and Lancashire; besides the warlike history of the place, I know nothing for which they are famous - except for their excellent Cheshire cheese, which they send in immense quantities to London.

One of the domestic habits of England is to make a servant girl wear a cap, always - an admirable idea - it keeps their hair from seasoning the food and makes them look tidy.

Chester being so different from any other town in England, seems determined to be so in every way, for its streets are badly lighted and it is the darkest and most melancholy town at night I have ever visited. As I now write, the night is relieved by the ringing of a deep toned and sweetly sounding bell, belonging I think to the Cathedral.

I am conscious that this town is worthy of a better notice than I give it in these papers, and I have therefore bought a guide book and some views to make up the deficiency.

In Liverpool the other day, I went to the Chapel of the Blind, where they are the musicians; they sang well, poor blind creatures who have not to thank Providence for sight. I felt for them - in their musical worship, I credited their sincerity, and was infected with their gratitude when they sang:

> Forgive me Lord for Thy dear Son
> The ills that I this day have done
> That with myself, the world and Thee
> I, ere I sleep, at peace may be.[31]

In a conversation with an intelligent farmer, he told me that the drill sowing suits best for light dry land, and the judicious draining has much enhanced the value of the land.

> He pays his best plowmen ten pounds and board per year.
> He pays his best dairy maid ten pounds and board per year.
> He pays his common women servants six pounds and board per year.

A good-natured fellow was my farmer friend, and only to recollect him I will record the following anecdote, which afforded him much mirth in telling it.

It seems that in days gone by, the terms of agreement between master and servant were to give the servant so much money and the rim of his knife (which means his board, and likely in those days the pocket knife was the table knife too, as I have known it to be in Scotland in my own time). So it appears, that a respectable and wealthy farmer had occasion to visit the lawyer once, and the lawyer insisted on his client becoming his guest to dinner, 'twas agreed. The lawyer was a good liver and a fashionable man. The dinner was in accordance, and a choice company of ladies and gentlemen sat down. Although everything was more stylish than the farmer had ever seen before, yet his good sense helped him and he got on very well until the liveried servant handed him the plate with some cheese cut up in small bits. It did not take the worthy farmer's fancy, who was accustomed to cut his own cheese, and in much larger pieces. So instead of accepting cheese from the servant, he drew from his pocket a large knife and turning to the affrighted servant, with great seriousness observed, "Zound thou see'st lad, I've got a knife of mine own." No doubt it amused the fashionables.

CHAPTER 8

Staffordshire

P otteries in Staffordshire. This is a most interesting region of country. The potteries, so called, cover a surface of land seven miles in length, by two miles in breadth, and in one continuous line of towns supported entirely by the manufacture of earthenware, china, and glassware. The situation is a good one for the purpose, as coal is very abundant, and canals to Liverpool, Manchester, Birmingham, and other parts of England run through this section of country, affording a cheap means for fetching the clay from Cornwall, Derby, and Kent, and for sending, when manufactured, the ware to market. And further, the local clay is excellent for making bricks and tile, while the cheapness of the coal permits the production of this useful material at a very low rate, and has been, most likely, the partial means of producing so many towns in such a small district and country, and by drawing together so many workmen, lively competition has resulted and enabled the manufacturers to bring to such perfection this branch of human industry. Although the place is as smoky as other manufacturing towns, the people are more bright, rosy, and healthful in their appearance, which leads me to imagine that smoke alone is not so unhealthy, and the loss of health, which is noticeable in many towns where manufacturing is the chief end, must arise from a number of causes. And judging from Glasgow and Liverpool, where the smoke becoming impregnated with a salt atmosphere from the sea, is dashed into your nostrils and skin, and observing that an unhealthy tinge marks the people of these two cities, I am inclined to believe that a variety of causes exist in manufacturing towns to cause ill health, independent of smoke, but a truce to nonsense. Today I spent in visiting the potteries of Wm. Davenport & Co., Minton & Co., and Alcock & Co., and will now try and describe what I saw and learned.

Although this is the seat of china and earthenware manufacture, yet there is not a particle of clay or stone used, but which has to be brought more than a hundred to two hundred miles. Cornwall clay and a particular Cornwall stone are used in the finer articles; but for the common, a mixture of other clays with the Cornwall is made, as the Derby and Kent and Devonshire clays are cheaper. Bones are used in china.

The first process is to put the clay into large troughs and beat it, mixed with water, into a liquid. This passes through brass wire sieves, finer than the finest muslin in its texture. It then runs into large vats and is boiled; then it runs into cooling troughs, where it becomes of the consistency of calf's foot jelly. This they cut up with a spade, in pieces about two feet square, which they throw into an iron mill. It passes twice through the mill and comes out at last free from wind or air bubbles, and so close in the fiber that the same bulk is nearly as weighty as iron. From the mill it goes to the work shop. Here it is worked by women as bread is baked, and given to the shaper in such quantities as he required for the vessel which he is about to make. And so well does everyone understand their part, that the quantity given is always exactly the quantity required to make the teapot, plate, or whatever it may be.

In this first room of shaping, a girl turns a large wheel; this gives motion to a perpendicular axle, on top of which is placed a wooden cap eight by twelve inches in diameter; a man sits opposite the cap; it is as high as a table usually is; when the girl gives him the clay he places it on the cap, and while this is rapidly revolving, he quickly shapes the vessel with only his hand, a small plate of iron, and his eye. Then the vessel is shaped and polished inside, which is done in less than a minute; he slips a thread under it which cuts it away from the small platform, and it is carried to the baking room. The baking room is a large dark room with shelves upon which the vessels are placed and remain subject to a warm temperature for twenty-four hours. They are then passed into the turning shop, there to be turned in a lathe and made very even and smooth on the outside. The vessel is made complete here by attaching handles if required; or if a plain vessel, like a plate, by giving the finish to the shape. And then all the vessels are placed in large common earthenware crocks; they are conveyed to the furnace, and as many are therein packed, as it will hold, each vessel cemented at the mouth, to make them air-tight. Then the furnace mouth is built up and the ware becomes subject for two or three days to an exceedingly hot temperature. When the vessels are taken out, they are pure white, an eighth smaller than when put in the furnace. After this, each vessel undergoes examination, and is scoured with sandpaper and sponges. Then it passes into the printing room; the figure to be printed is on copper. From these plates, which are coated with the color and a particular gum mixture, sheets of paper are struck off, which a girl picks up and places on the vessel to be printed, and arranging it properly, she rubs it into the ware with a bit of leather. The vessel is then dipped in a tub of water, and with a sponge the paper is washed off, and behold, the print remains perfect on the vessel. If only one color is required, the ware is now ready for the glaze, but if more than one color is required, the ware passes in another room, where the additional colors are given and filled in with the brush and paint. To make all this permanent and to turn the biscuit surface into a hard and lasting one, it passes to the glazing room. The glaze is a white liquid, composed of borax, arsenic, lead, and some other ingredients. Into this compound the ware is dipped; when taken out, it is as white as 'twas before being printed or painted. As soon as dry, it is again placed in coarse jars or vessels and again sent to the furnace, where it is subject to an air tight heat for eighteen hours. When taken out, the white glaze has become glass; the printing and painting clear and distinct through the glaze, and the vessel is in its finished state as seen in use.

When the ware is packed in jars for the furnace, little clay crotchets are placed between each dish; these stick and leave little rough points where they touched the ware. These rough points are rubbed off by the girls, with steel instruments. If common ware, it then goes to the warehouse for packing in crates, but if china or finer ware with ornaments or gold, a finishing process has yet to come.

In making china ware with gold, the gold is mixed with silver, arsenic, and some other materials, which make a black paint. This is painted on the china where it is wanted; then it is sent to the furnace, which burns off everything except the gold. The gold is then burnished with the gold stone until it is perfectly bright, when the finish is complete in that article.

In ornamental vases, figures, or designs, when flowers, wreaths, etc. are planned, there is much hard labor and ingenuity. And so ingenious have they become, that they make beautiful lace of clay, which would defy the most practical eye to discover not to be lace. This lace they place on their figures in biscuit ware, and make the deception complete. Yet so fragile is the fabric, that the touch of the finest camel's hair brush would annihilate the lace into nothing.

Besides the articles made into shape by the hand, yet many articles are made in molds, as jugs and vessels of china, figures, etc.

Designers, painters, and artists of the rarest ability are employed in the potteries.

Show rooms (themselves beautiful), filled with the rarest and most chaste samples of their manufacturing skill, are here - containing so much that is beautiful and excellent that the mind and taste are completely bewildered.

I saw some dinner sets of china for some of the nobles of this land, which were to cost 1,000 pounds, or 5,000 pounds for the set. This brings the single plate at fifteen pounds – rather too dear for the Buffalo market.

If the samples I bought reach the United States in good order, they will prove to my friends the fine skill of the potteries. Where will human ingenuity stop when such wealth and beauty is brought out of clay?

A new pattern of stone ware is now the rage. It is a blue which appears to partially melt and run into the white. This is to imitate the ancient china and is brought about by sprinkling a handful of salt in the bottom of the jar which contains the ware when sent to furnace with the glaze. The action of the heat on the salt impregnates the atmosphere just enough to make the blue run, but before it has run too far the heat has fixed the glaze, and the paint becomes guarded from any further effect from the salt.

> Minton & Co.[32]
> Copeland & Garrett[33]
> Alcock & Co.[34]
> Wm. Davenport & Co.[35]

Are the finest manufacturers, especially the first two named.

The two unhealthy parts in the manufacture of china and earthenware are, first, the rubbing and sconing with sandpaper etc. of the ware after it leaves the first firing; the dust, which is the grains of clay, stone, and flint, go up the nostrils and in at the eyes, producing early death. Next is the glazing – the parties who dip the ware inhale a solution of arsenic, lead, borax, etc.; nervous destruction and early death follow.

Besides the mills for driving the air bubbles from the clay and tightening the fiber, they have runs of stones for grinding bones, lead, and Cornwall stone in liquid state, which is in making the glaze.

The kindness of Messrs. Davenport & Co., Alcock & Co., Mr. Robert Stevenson, lawyer Hawley, Mr. John Stevenson, lawyer Stoke, and Mr. James Stevenson of Liverpool, made my visit to the potteries valuable, interesting, and agreeable; and, although a place where I knew nobody before, yet I find I have contracted an addition to the debt of gratitude which I owe in this country for kindness and hospitality.

CHAPTER 9

Stockport and Manchester

February 13. Today I saw another wonder in this wonderful country of man's ingenuity: a railroad built over a city on arches a mile and a half in width, and the houses away below us. 'Twas a novel sight and somewhat startling to find yourself in mid-air in a railway train, flying at the speed of thirty or forty miles per hour.[36] The town alluded to is Stockport, and so dense was the atmosphere of smoke that it created an atmosphere between us and the houses so thick that we could scarcely distinguish them, and fancy might have pictured us riding above the clouds.

Manchester, February 15, 1844. In the following remarks, I am about to describe the process which cotton goes through before it becomes ready for market in a manufactured state. These remarks must fall short of a full description, for it is the result of only one visit, and the proprietors take care not to allow you to tarry too long, for much jealousy exists, and it required the very strong letters which I carried to obtain admission at all.

The first mill spun the cotton and wove it, no more. This mill was ten stories high and contained 1,450 work people. Apart from the interest to be felt in examining minutely the different steps of manufacturing, and enjoying the ingenious mechanism by which labor is nearly abolished, it is indeed a wonderful sight to enter a room eighty feet wide by two hundred feet long, completely covered with machines, leaving only a very narrow passage between every double row of machines, with one girl attending to every two machines; these machines covered with a forest of spindles set a-dancing by the long line of machinery overhead; the girls turning from one machine to the other; the spindles constantly whirling, and the endless deep humming and gurgling din of the machinery – is enough to bewilder the clearest head. It is an incomparable sight, and when the attention turns from the grand view to things in detail, the pleasure and wonder is only increased, you cease to be surprised at the results, for you see in the peculiar application and adaptation of one part of a machine to the other, and the certain working perfection of the combination sufficient to enable you to grasp the cause of the grand result - you cease to wonder, but continue to admire.

The first room contains machines for cleaning the cotton, which is done by drawing it through rollers into a pan or box, where every particle of black speck and all foreign substance is blown and worked out of it. It passes from the pan through rollers and comes out in sheets like batting, about thirty inches wide and rolled on rollers to the thickness of two feet in diameter – and is passed on these rollers to the second room.

The second room contains the carding and drawing machines. The wool enters the cards from the roller and continues its width of about thirty inches; after passing through the cards it is drawn together to a point and passes through a round aperture of about half an inch diameter, and then in company with a similar roll or sliver from neighboring machines (nine in number) pass along a narrow tin trough (which is placed across the end of the line of machines) until the nine slivers all enter one small set of rollers, which rollers seize the wool and, with the force of gunpowder, actually drives nine slivers through an aperture again, one-half inch in diameter; in front of this aperture stands a tin tub three feet deep; over this tub hangs a cap open at side next where the wool comes, from which cap the wool continues to ascend and descend quickly, so as to drive the wool down into the tub or can.

I may here remark that when the cotton left the card it was about thirty inches wide and half an inch thick. This is drawn down to half an inch in diameter, and then nine of these drawn down together to about half an inch diameter.

Ten cans of these slivers are placed beside another machine which seizes the end of all at once and draws the whole ten down to the size of twine. All this is done without any spinning or twisting – nine are drawn together and ten of the products of nine which makes ninety times reduced.

The object of all this drawing is to straighten the thread or rather the fibers of the cotton, which the cleaning and carding had disturbed. This compound operation of drawing prepares the cotton for spinning in a state wherein every fiber or hair of the cotton is straight and laying side by side. This fetches us to the third room – wherein they spin the cotton into thread; and here is the most ingenious machine of all. The "spinning wheel" is a machine which spins 450 to 600 threads at once on different spindles and requiring only one little girl to attend to the whole machine. A room containing twenty of these machines with only twenty women to attend them will spin more thread in the same time than ten thousand women could with the hand wheel! What change is this! The machine is somewhat like an upright piano on the front of which would be placed row above row of spindles covered with cotton in a drawn state, ready for spinning. From these spindles the cotton proceeds downwards and running through small apertures about where the fingers of the piano are, attach to another spindle which is on the outside of the frame. To carry out the metaphor, suppose the part of the piano which is forward of perpendicular of the back, to be on wheels, which by the action of machinery would run out, say ten feet, making the thread follow and twist quickly all the while; and fancy the part which ran out on wheels after it got so far out, of its own accord run back again and, as it ran back, twist the thread which it has just made, on to the spindle which was on the outside of the piano. In running back an instrument operates on two rows of wires, which compel the thread to coil regularly on the spindle to which it is transferred, so it keeps moving forward and backward, taking the thread from one spindle, twisting it and placing it on another, ready for the loom. The machinery which makes the outside spindle twirl around and draw the cotton from inside spindles, is under the framework. A cord like the string of a piano goes round each spindle, and about twenty of them go round a perpendicular drum which is always in motion, and acts and moves with the machine.

We now come to the fourth room, where the roving machines are; here the spindles are deprived of the thread, which is rove onto a roller about thirty inches wide; enough is put on one roller to make 360 yards of cloth. We now pass to the finish, namely the fifth room, where the thread is made into cloth by the power loom, which is again self-acting, and only one girl attends two or three machines or looms at once. Each loom makes 36 yards per day – which to three looms is 108 yards for a child's one day's work. To place the warp takes about two hours for each 360 yards then the shuttle with its thread moves from side to side with the velocity of lightning – and the operation is complete, for as it weaves it coils on to another roller, which moves with the machine, and finally passes to the folding room, where it is taken from rollers and folded into pieces preparatory to going to market as brown sheeting, or to bleaching and printing works to become calico.

Before transferring my thoughts to the printing process, which is a different branch of manufacture and carried on by different persons in separate establishments, I must dwell upon the establishment a little longer, whose operation I have just been describing. A building containing fifteen hundred of our fellow creatures and these mostly women, commands our strongest sympathy and interest. So high was the house that the people are hoisted up in a bucket, dozens at a time, to the different floors. And there in rooms where everything is in the most perfect order, and without any visible overseer, you find so many of our creatures working out their destiny. What can I say? What am I to think on the subject? Alas! I am at a loss! Are they happy? I answer – no! Are they sorrowful or miserable? I answer - no! But they are cheerful, thoughtless, tolerably healthful, and pass their existence, if not with exalted consciousness, at least contentedly – too much life in their eye for apathy. Earnest and incessant attention is required to the machinery which they tend, not a moment for thought or other subject, hence they, on their day's labor being done, feel they have done their duty – and I should question their mental ability or inclinated to think then. Supper and frolic they no doubt consider their due after having done what they deem their sum of their duty to man, themselves, and perhaps their God. Poor girls – I do not grieve for their physical lot, it is their very contentment that pains me. They know little of real rational pleasure or pain; it is their lot to suffer neither – their existence and fate is in the hands of our common God, who no doubt has a care for them as he has for us; under the present state of society perhaps their lot is for the best.

I have already said that the printing and bleaching of calico or cotton cloth is a business by itself – let us visit such an establishment.

The first room is a room of receipts – full of cloth fit for calico, muslin de laine,[37] shawls and handkerchiefs, all colorless as yet.

The second room is the firing room, where the cloth is twice passed over a roller of red-hot iron, and, strange to say, this operation is performed without affecting the fabric in the least, beyond singeing of the furze, which is the object of the operation. As the cloth passes over the roller, smoking, blazing, and yet not burning, it is rapidly rolled on to another roller – in which state it passes to the third room, which is the bleaching room. This is performed in a very summary manner. The cloth passes through rollers, descending passes under another roller, which is submerged in a solution of bleaching powder, etc.; it ascends, and as it passes through the next set of rollers, the bleaching liquid is squeezed out, while the cloth passes round merely to be submerged again; this process is continued for about two hours – during which time the cloth becomes perfectly white. It then passes through strainers or rollers, which are filled with steam; this dries them and they pass to the printing house.

To dry goods of the finest texture and which are to be of best printing, a scientific method has been adopted. A copper vat or box – its center containing a perpendicular shaft on which the vat revolves – this center casing eighteen inches to two feet in diameter, is surrounded by another wall of copper, which wall is pierced with very small holes all over; the distance being about eighteen inches between the center casing and this outside wall, while the depth is about two to three feet. All this is cased in cast iron of strong fiber, having both air-tight cover and grating above, making the whole strong and air-tight (except at the bottom) all over. Between the center drum and the inside casing, which I remarked as pierced with small holes, the wet cloth fresh from the bleaching room, is placed – as much as it can hold (perhaps 100 pieces 30 yards) - tied in bundles of about one dozen; the copper cover is then put on, over this is a wrought iron grating is tightly fastened and the whole vat set in motion; round it goes on its perpendicular shaft with the speed of lightning; its velocity or centrifugal force is so great that it forces the cloth against the outside wall which is pierced with holes, and through these holes the water is forced, thence passing through the bottom by an aperture between the copper (hole) side and the cast iron casing. In two minutes the operation is performed, the cloths which were as much as the place would hold are now so compressed around the outer side, that the space around the drum is half the size of the whole apartment, and the result is that the cloth is removed perfectly dry. Another triumph of science and art combined.

After the burning, bleaching, and drying, the cloth all passes through rollers and is (stitched about 100 pieces together) rolled on to rollers, which rollers with the cloth on them are carried to the prints room. This we will call the fifth room, where the printing begins. Three colors can be printed at once by rollers, provided the colors do not mingle; for instance – the cloth passing over one roller will receive a sprig or flower of blue, over another roller a green line will cross the cloth between each row of flowers; over another roller a yellow line will run the length of the cloth, making by this style, a green and yellow check with a blue flower or sprig. Before going further with this process, I will define how so much is brought about. The rollers are of copper on the surface of which is engraved some particular figure; as this roller revolves it is partly submerged in the mixture of color required; its revolution continues over a tight cloth which rubs off all the color except that retained in the engraved parts, which is fixed in the cloth to be printed as it quickly passes over the roller on the other side. If additional colors are required, they have to be put on with wooden blocks by hand. This is done in another room, which we will call the sixth room – with long tables on which the cloth is spread as required. Beside each table is a railway on which a boy slides a box (same height as the table); the bottom is of thick felt cloth; this the lad continues to rub over with the color, and on this the printer feeds his wooden block for each new impression; if to give a rainbow color or lines of blue green etc., alternately side by side. The cloth which the boy supplies is so fed that by a gauge he has the colors planted properly and when the printer replenishes his block he can rely on its having on its face the very hues he wishes to plant on the calico or cloth as it may be called.

Borders of shawls of cotton are all printed by blocks, and all goods which do not have continuous figures.

The difference between the figures on the block and on the copper roller is that on the first, the figure required is raised - on the copper it is sunk; still both act the same, with this difference, that the stamp from the block is never so sharp as from the copper and sometimes looks as if it ran a little.

Seventh room – Here all the goods after being printed are brought to be washed – if they are intended to be fast colors, they are submerged by rollers in a madder solution and become what is called madder or part colors. Then in company with the others they go to be washed. This is done by putting them into cased waterwheels, through holes for that purpose in the side of the wheel. The wheel is half full of water and is half submerged in water which keeps running out and in. These wheels revolve with rapidity, and the friction of the cloth washes the cloth. It is taken out, rolled smooth, and passes to the starch and steam drying roller. As the cloth enters the first rollers it passes through a pool of starch which the rollers again squeeze out of it or nearly all. The cloth continues through a dozen other rollers, of barrel size and constantly filled with steam; as it moves it dries. From this the cloth goes to the eighth room.

This is the steaming room. Near the ceiling are spans on which the cloth is hung all over the room – the floor of which is only grating through which proceeds a strong head of steam. This continues for twenty-four hours and fetches out the colors on the cloth so as to make them appear to greater advantage and brilliance. From this room they are moved to one higher up, with a similar floor, only that is covered with blankets; the heat of the steaming room below passes through the blanket, but not the steam. Iron pipes encircle the room, heated by steam, and in this atmosphere the cloth continues to hang about a day, when the colors are considered set and the cloth ready for folding and sale.

Such variety of patterns have to be printed that it requires a very large stock of copper rollers for such an establishment of 600 persons, as I have just been describing. Such stock may be valued at 10,000 pounds, and as this is only one item, the building machinery and fixtures may be considered worth 150,000 pounds to 200,000 pounds, and of such establishments there are hundreds here.

The engraver's shop of the establishment is most interesting. Here they make the patterns on the copper rollers, from which the cloth is printed. This is done by making a steel roller of small size, fit to make one line of figures on the copper roller. To make this, they take the temper from the steel, put on the figure or etching or lining required; then the temper is brought back to the steel, the copper roller is placed in a lathe, the small steel roller acts on a part of the surface of the roller, and the steel roller moves as it does its work. This is so far finished; now deeper figures have to be made, therefore the copper roller receives a coat of varnish of a particular character which withstands vitriol or any acid. This varnish is only placed in the raised parts; on the engraved or etched parts there is no varnish put. When this varnish is dry, the whole roller gets a coat of acid; it eats into those parts of the copper not varnished and makes the required depth. When rollers are worn, they are ground smooth and cut over again.

The temper is taken from steel by placing it in an iron vessel with burned bone. This is cemented and immersed in a strong tin for twenty-four hours. The temper is brought back by nearly a similar process only in half the time.

I may as well note that the steel rollers are only able to cut lines on the copper; for flowers the figure is taken from the steel on cloth or paper. This is impressed on the copper after it is lined; and then the chisel, following the impression, does the rest. A most tedious job, which is so much so, as with the assistance of acid requiring two, three, or sometimes four weeks to make one roll perfect. And so minutely has it to be done, that the naked eye dare not be trusted; hence the workmen look through a magnifying glass while they ply their tool.

I notice a street cleaning cart here - the body is covered - under the cart, leaning out behind is a set of brushes, within which are small buckets; these revolve by the action of a crank, which works on another crank on the inside of a wheel, all of which is moved by the motion of the cart - so that the horse walks and cleans and shovels and carries away as he proceeds – for the brushes revolve inwardly and upwardly, throwing the dust into the little bucket, which proceeds upward and disgorges itself into the cart, and proceeds downward again for another load.

From the potteries to Sandbach I rode through a beautiful agricultural country – the cattle, the houses, the hedges, and the parks all so beautiful and refreshing – many of the farm houses had the age on the outside, appearing as built in 1600 or 1650 – built of framework and filled in with brick; plastered and painted white, the wood divisions black, sharp gables, odd windows – altogether antique.

CHAPTER 10

Sandbach, York, and Sheffield

~ ~~ ~

Sandbach - a pretty, old-fashioned little country town; bless its simplicity, see its marketplace, then in the cross to indicate it, a crown to a penny - but that cross has stood there these five hundred years;[38] what a fine old church, seven or eight hundred years old, I'll be bound! Ah! How much joy, sorrow, and death has that old church covered, and if its spirit or genius would speak, how I could listen!

Since that old church was built, science has taught us much; art has produced many things that our forefathers did not know, and mankind are far better traders or shopkeepers than the people who worshipped in the venerable old church of Sandbach in gone by ages - but that the present generation are wiser or better or happier with their knowledge, I cannot believe.

The finest evidence of human happiness to be seen in England is in a country town of an agricultural district, in every look, in every word, in every action you perceive modesty, respectfulness, independence, honesty, and chastened joyfulness, which shows a clean conscience, an honest purpose, and trust in God.

I do not feel that I can say the same for the manufacturing towns. Radicalism and the want of <u>church</u> influence has made the newspaper become the Bible, and vanity of heart, I fear, makes many think little of God or His church.

A very picturesque and pretty farming country between Manchester and Hull; Halifax, Huddersfield, Rochdale, Leeds, Wakefield, and Selby are all nice towns, the two last are rural – and both have very fine churches. While Wakefield is distinguished as a great grain market, the other towns are entirely engrossed with cloth and woolen manufacture.

I remarked to a Quaker gentleman at Selby – "What a fine old church, if it could only speak, what tales it would tell!" "Yes," said the Quaker, "but they would be more of darkness than of light." And so the world goes! All think their own persuasion and opinions the true ones, and all others false or erroneous. One would think a little more charity and less sectarianism would improve the tone of society.

Hull is pleasantly situated, of much importance as a seaport town, and like every other town almost, which I have visited, the old church is the principal Lion in the place.

York is a walled city, a great part of the wall in fine condition, a magnificent castle, rebuilt lately, covering a large extent of ground. Many old churches of much interest to the traveler; the ruins of St. Mary's Abbey; a Museum of Antiques, as stone coffers, etc., and the grandest cathedral man ever set eyes upon, and to add still to this the finest looking inhabitants – best made and most beautiful women, of the most graceful carriage and taste in dress of any I have yet seen in England.

I feel, as I write, that in noting my opinion of York and all therein, that if I write as I feel I would appear hereafter in my own view as a creature overwhelmed with ridiculous enthusiasm, and if I put down in a cold phlegmatic style my remarks on York, they will be no true journal of impression. I will do neither – the visit will remain strongly marked in my mind without record on paper.

I will recollect the Cathedral with its hundred painted windows, its monuments, its arches, its columns, its statues beheaded by Cromwell,[39] its Apostles and Virgin of silver, stolen by some person, its founder, DeGray and his tomb,[40] the screenery, the choir, the Lady Chapel, the Chair one thousand years old, the Chapter House, with its figures of nuns and monks in its eight fine stained glass windows and hundreds of stalls; the great size, nearly a mile in circumference; in short, all of the hundreds of beauties of this ancient and most elegant structure I cannot soon forget.

Nor can I forget Saint Mary's Abbey, although in time the gorgeous architecture, the great size, covering two other acres, the stone coffins, the monumental sculpture, and the chaste museum built within its ruins.

Nor can I forget the odd old churches – and so many of them – their fine, carved doorways all moldering under a thousand years' use, and still the places of worship, where the inhabitants meet to praise their God as their forefathers did a thousand years before. Surely such buildings must become hallowed by being the altar of thanksgiving of God's creatures for so many generations.

Nor can I forget the queer fashioned old houses and streets, so narrow that the cats jump from the roofs on one side of the street to those of the other – and then I will think how these old houses were the scene of revelry, mirth, joy, sorrow, and pain to people such as ourselves, who have been dust for hundreds of years, and whom we must follow by and by. Houses stand for ages, but man soon passes away – even brick and mortar of our own creation laugh our vanity to scorn, and tell mortals that when his time, which so soon arrives, does come, he must pass away and nobody be missed. "And yet 'tis sad to think, 'twill be the same when we are gone."

Nor will I forget the fine form and beautiful faces of the ladies of York; their grace, action, chaste and beautiful dress, education and refinement – 'tis a rare place, this old town; no trade, no manufacturing disturbs its inhabitants – its old Cathedral, a model of the most exalted taste, has modeled its inhabitants' minds for many a day, and the hallowing influences of quiet, yet refined religion shows itself in every face.

Sheffield. In the neighborhood of this town there are several objects of interest, as Chatsworth House and Haddon Hall. The town itself is no great attraction; it is only a work shop wherein labor is so much divided and subdivided, that every house looks like a manufactory. The people seem to have little intercourse with other parts of England, and stare at a stranger as if he were a prodigy whose likes they might never see again. Nor are they a good-looking people, either; they seem diminutive in stature, sallow in complexion, and spare in flesh. The merchant manufacturers of the town are respectable and sensible men, but refinement, superior education, or fine intelligence – it is very rare here, as far as my limited observations can judge. The great body of the people are Methodists, and many of the higher class also. The Church has but a small hold here, and the want of her refining influence is visible.

The want of high breeding and superior intelligence is not the only trouble here; for the very law is powerless; every respectable man is the slave of his own workmen – and to attempt to be free from such thralldom would set your property on fire, or fetch down even in a worse way (perhaps by murder) your rebellious thoughts to a level with the demagogues of the workshop, who rule here triumphant. If Sheffield had but fifty strong, clear, and educated men, of standing and influence in society, I think the present state of things would not be allowed to long exist; but all are plodders, think more for themselves than for aught else, and will continue to do so until the town has lost its trade, and what heretofore has been a growing and flourishing town, will become a ruinous pile of brick and mortar.

The scenery around Sheffield is very good, a high and undulating country, divided between cultivation and moor land, with here and there a rocky eminence for the eye to rest upon. The only public building of note in Sheffield is the Methodist Proprietary School; it is the best in England, is built in the Corinthian and Roman order of architecture, at a great expense; of great dimensions, beautiful arrangement, and admirably furnished – with furniture, kitchens, drawing rooms, school rooms, lecture rooms, chapel with an organ, play grounds – swimming, hot and vapid baths, etc.[41] The object is to fully educate youths, and at the same time instruct and strengthen them in Methodism. I understand the establishment is in a very flourishing condition, yet am free to confess that the Principals whom I saw were vulgar, ignorant, half parson, half school master sort of folks, to whose care I would be very loath to send any child whom I wished to become a refined and educated being.

My Methodist friend, while showing me the school, related the following interesting story:

Some ladies clubbed together to elucidate the Scriptures to each other; when they arrived at that part where life truths are shadowed forth as the refiner of silver, they resolved to visit a refiner and ask him to explain the manner of refining silver; he answered them thus: "When the silver is in the crucible and under the action of the fire, I watch it as it boils, sitting constantly overlooking the process – when the metal is at a certain point my face becomes distinctly reflected in the fluid, and then I know that the silver is pure and refined and it is immediately withdrawn from the crucible."[42]

CHAPTER 11

Chatsworth House

T he ride from Sheffield to Chatsworth is pleasant; as you near the latter place it is wild and grand, for this is the land of the peak. Wild and savage rocks standing out boldly above all around, deep valleys – without any agreeable relief from scene of rock, mountain, and heather until, all at once, as if from another world, you pass the lodge of the Duke of Devonshire's Park, and, sure enough! The scene is changed, the very atmosphere is warmer here, to be in keeping with this lovely and magnificent domain. And now we are about to attempt the description of one of England's noblest mansions. Such a mansion as a prince would envy, large enough to house and entertain three thousand people. 'Tis indeed a fairy scene as you pass through the spacious domain of many thousand acres, studded with venerable old oaks, beneath which flocks of deer are browsing. Now we approach the mansion. Why! Look at that elegant gate and porch. Can it be gold, or is it plated? Either way, how pretty it looks; the style of the house purely Italian – so chaste yet gorgeous, what an extent of ground it covers – but let us enter. Oh! Oh! Can this be a dining room? No, it is only the entrance chamber; the ceiling is one gorgeous sculptural painting. The floor is beautiful marble. Alas! Alas! How can I methodically describe such a place. 'Tis impossible! The ceiling and walls of every room elegantly adorned with paintings by first artists of many ages, the floors of oak polished to the brilliance of a mirror. The tapestry sometimes takes the place of paintings on the wall and marble sometimes the place of oak on the floor.

The library is large, every book richly bound, beautifully ranged and sumptuously cased, the statuary filling a whole room and parts of many rooms, of finest artists and best subjects. The galleries of paintings and pencilings – where many paintings were valued at 20,000 pounds each. The windows, gold plated frames outside and in, with only one pane of glass in each, and that glass impossible to be distinguished with the naked eye at a distance of three feet.

The chapel, so chaste and holy – it looked like all else – so gorgeous. The chairs of state in which William and Adelaide[43] were crowned – all, all in this wonderful house so grand, so chaste, so beautiful, and so costly, that a month's examination would scarcely allow time for a proper description. I only saw enough to astonish me, and so great was my surprise that, though I have seen other noble mansions, yet my notions fell far short of what I here beheld, and I could but look, wonder, and enjoy.

And was this mansion, now so lovely, the prison of my own country's Queen – Mary Stuart?[44] Indeed, it was. Here she remained for many a day, and in the park – a rifle shot from the palace – stands the old elevated bower where she was sometimes allowed to breathe the fresh air. Never do I think of poor Queen Mary Stuart but I shed a sigh to her memory.

When you leave the house, the water works first attract attention; they are very pretty – but the greatest object of attraction out of the house is the conservatory, which is a round building covering three acres of ground and built entirely of glass from the foundation to the top. It contains every rarity of flower, trees from every clime, and displays a degree of taste which is gigantic and correct at the same time. Her Majesty, to satisfy her curiosity, came all the way from London, chiefly to see this conservatory. She drove through it in her carriage; at night 'twas illuminated with three thousand Roman lights, and must have been grand.

Besides the conservatory there is about one hundred acres of garden, in which there is nearly two miles of hot houses growing peaches, pineapples, grapes, etc., and the gardener told me that they never wanted for any of these fruits, summer or winter. He showed me one small tree which the Duke had sent a person to India for – at a cost of some 3,000 pounds.

To finish this tame description or rather apology for a description, I may remark that the Duke's income is 300,000 pounds per annum, one-third of which he has spent on Chatsworth and the grounds each year for the past thirty years – for he is deeply in debt even with this large revenue. I almost forgot to allude to his farming village, which is about a mile from the palace. It is a little walled city of ancient Saxon style of buildings, with its church and schoolhouse and parsonage – every house fit for a gentleman of moderate fortune to reside in. In a conversation with a working man in the village, I said, "Who lives in these fine houses?" "We do." "Then," I said, "You must be very happy?" "Oh yes, but there is a deal too much trumpery about them." Poor fellow, I envied him in his independence from taste and appearance, for he evidently would have been quite as contented in a mud hovel, if it was clean.

The lodge at this end of the park was beautiful, of oak, varnished and oiled on the outside, and the brick filling painted a claret red; 'twas unique and pretty. I saw at some distance a fine cut-stone house being built; I asked if it was for a neighboring gentleman, and found that it was for the Duke's head gamekeeper.

When the late Duchess of Devonshire was "enceinte"[45] she bargained with a lady of high degree, who was an intimate friend of hers and who was in the same state as the Duchess, that whoever had a male child, he was to be Duke of Devonshire. It so happened that the Duchess had a girl, the change was therefore made, and with so much secrecy that the Duchess died and the present occupant was forty years of age and in possession of the estates for a long time before it was found out that he was not the real Duke; but it is understood that he made a compact with the Cavendish family – who are the real owners – that he remains Duke of Devonshire for life on consideration of his not marrying – the Duke is now about 55 years old.[46]

CHAPTER 12

Haddon Hall

Fu rom Chatsworth House we proceeded to Haddon Hall, considered the finest old-fashioned baronial mansion in England.
'Tis finely situated; a lovely river winds below its walls, full of trout; a
range of hills rise quickly behind it - itself on the edge of a valley. No
one now lives in it, although it is in a state of great preservation, and
if fires were only put in it, it would last for many centuries to come.

This was the stronghold of the Vernons, one of the most powerful
families England boasted of. The last of the name were two sisters,
one of whom married a Manners, by which the family name became
extinct and Duke of Rutland (a Manners) is now the owner and representative of this old mansion and its ancient owners, the Vernons.

The first thing on entering the courtyard that struck the eye, was the
lodge where we saw two pairs of old boots with immense heels and
very square at the toes, a helmet, a sword, a fine coat of mail, likewise
the horn, on which I blew a blast; many of the old pewter plates were

here also. We next passed into the chapel, a queer old Romish place with its confessional, holy water vase, painted windows and old pews, desk, and pulpit. When it became Protestant under the Reformation, it did not appear necessary to this noble Vernon, to destroy man's art and ingenuity – and thanks to him, all is now as it was a thousand years ago. From the chapel we went to the dining hall, a fine old room, high roof, the rafters uncovered, so as Burns said, when in their flagons of ale they must have "made the rafters ring."

A gallery was around on one side, entrance to which was obtained from other parts of the house, and where the ladies no doubt occasionally sat watching the enjoyments of their lords.

The fireplace was very large, with immense andirons, much superior in fashion to those of the present day, where no doubt they piled the immense logs which illuminated the whole hall while they ate.

The kitchens were very near the hall; against the wall there was a handcuff in which anyone was imprisoned who refused to drink as much as his neighbor – that was a sum teetotal society. Some old paintings hang on the walls, of huntsmen, etc. We passed to the drawing rooms, enveloped in tapestry, the sofas and chairs and tables still there – dear old things; then to the state bedrooms. There we saw the two chairs in which Henry the VII and VIII were crowned. Thence we passed to the ballroom, and such a ballroom – its long oak polished floor, its deep windows, fit to hold fifty people without interfering with the floor, and its little anterooms – altogether, the beau ideal of a dancing room.

From the ballroom we passed to the bedroom of Queen Elizabeth, and there still stands the bed, sheets, coverlid, curtains, and besides, a room of the most beautiful tapestry. I have seen the bed of Mary Queen of Scots, and now that of her successful rival, Queen Elizabeth. They are both before their God and each has received her due. They lived in harsh times, the good God would deal kindly with them for they both had much that was good in them. Two women who set the world ablaze – and then went out themselves.

From this apartment we rambled all over and under the old hall, found many rooms with fine tapestry and all in excellent preservation. The oak floors and wainscot seem as fresh as ever; the stone stairs are worn hollow with the footsteps of a thousand years and more; the turrets, the battlements, the tower - all are in order.

As I wandered about the dear old house, away from the guide and my friends, I lost myself in the labyrinth of rooms and halls. I became drunk with excitement, I laughed, shouted, danced, and went on from place to place like one possessed. One moment I fancied myself holding an audience with Elizabeth. I saw the fire in her haughty eye and felt that I stood in the presence of my superior. Then I recollected her bed with its gorgeous curtains, which I had just seen, and then I recollected that I was alone. Now I believed myself in the banquet hall, around me I saw a hundred knights fresh from the fray, fine fellows, too, black faces, red faces - aye - and one or two young clear faces (young Vernons I'll be bound) not yet seasoned with exposure and the flagon, but stern courage and noble kindness beaming from those eyes. Give me a flagon and I'll give you a toast - "The days of old! We shall never see their like again!" My own laugh ringing in my ear reminded me that a thousand years divided me and my banquet friends. But soon I was lost again - now I am in the drawing room; the ladies with their high frills and hooped dresses, bid me stand off, but still they look so kindly on me I venture near. Now I am all right, I have given my hand to Dorothy Vernon and the noble dame steps out to the ballroom, with a majestic mien. Look at the room as we enter, see the hundred noble knights who would not yield to a dozen enemies; how they bow in homage to the high-bred girls - yes, they almost touch the dust. Now the dance is formed, the music strikes up, but, alas! 'tis the laugh of my friends. Dorothy has left me; hundreds of years divide us, and I am again in the world of the Nineteenth Century.[47]

To know that on these chairs and sofas sat many a noble dame and lovely woman hundreds of years ago; in these chairs, kings were crowned; through these halls which I now tread, beings like ourselves, with similar passions, walked a thousand years ago. 'Tis being on hallowed ground; 'tis holding converse with the other world; 'tis ennobling, 'tis glorious! The dear old place, how I love it; its gardens, its ivy bowers, its old trees, its parterre. I will see them often for many years; and for many a night I will dream of those I saw in my day dream in Haddon Hall. The boar and the peacock are now united, but the peacock desired a more fanciful mansion than the old hall, and the boar, being a female, has been coaxed away from the old place.[48] 'Tis now cold and dreary, but at night it may still be warmed, when the spirits of old revisit our earth and take our nightly banquet. Indeed, it is agreeable to fancy such although we cannot believe. Old hall, your owners left you for a finer place; I, too, must leave you for my places.

From Haddon Hall we went to Bakewell for dinner. While the meal was being cooked, I sought out the lions of the place and found them to be a noble church, fine Roman baths,[49] and Bakewell pudding.[50] I did justice to all, entered our carriage at ten o'clock at night, and found ourselves once more in Sheffield.

CHAPTER 13

Rotherham

Rotherham is in the neighborhood of Sheffield. I found it a lively grain market, and iron and steel manufacturing going on cheerily. Here as elsewhere the grand church is the chief point of attraction. From this place I walked to Parkgate Ironworks,[51] the property of my friend, William Scholefield, Esq., [52]where I saw minutely the whole process of turning minerals into metals ready for use. Iron stone and iron ore, lime, and coal are the ingredients from which iron is produced. The iron stone is calcined; this is done by setting large piles on fire covered over with coal, then into the smelting furnace you pour first a quantity of coal, then put in your calcined iron stone and your iron ore, after that put in lime and coal as fast as consumed, always keeping the furnace full; this is done by hoisting all the ore, lime, and coal to the top of the furnace and then emptying it through holes on each side of the chimney; when the metal etc. melts, the pure iron sinks to the bottom, and the refuse floats on top. There are two taps; from the upper one they draw the refuse, and from the lower the iron. The refuse, when run out into the sand, makes cakes of a beautiful bronze color; this is taken away and broken up to make roads. Before drawing the iron, they prepare molds in the sand into which it runs and becomes pig iron. In melting the ore and iron stone with such a body of coal and lime, it is evident that an immense draft of wind is necessary to produce a requisite and constant heat; instead of blowing in cold air, they now send in hot air by the principle called the hot air blast. It is a simple contrivance although an advantage of immense importance. The pipe through which the air is pumped has to pass through a furnace which keeps that part of the pipe red hot, and as the air passes through this it becomes heated and passes into the iron furnace in that state, producing the desired draft without taking away from the temperature of the furnace.

Having got the ore into pig, we now turn it to the puddling of same; but first must turn the coal into cake; this is done by making large piles on the ground leaving some small channels for the draft, a small brick chimney is built in the center and then the whole is covered with an adhesive gravel which keeps the air out and retains the carbonatic with a virture in the coke. When the coal is red it is desirable that the fire should cease as soon as possible, for the heat is all that is requisite to take from the fuel certain sulphur compounds which are injurious in making iron.

The puddling furnace receives its quantity of pig iron and coke, and all is melted to a fearful heat, the scum is drawn off and then the liquid iron is taken out in large lumps, as much as a man can lift. It sticks together as they roll it on to a bar of iron and by this bar of iron they carry it up to the trip hammer, where it is hammered into shape and carried to the rollers which roll it down gradually to any length or thickness.

These bars are cut up and a number laid together; they are again subjected to a strong heat until they glue together; in this state they are rolled into one bar or sheet as may be required, then the stamp is put on and the article is ready for market.

The rollers for bars and boiler plate are very fine at these works and all in admirable order. Mr. Dysart, the manager, seems to be a clever fellow in doing everything he does well, and makes those under him to do likewise. I felt much pleased with his attention. Finding him making an iron cart, I suggested to him the propriety of making iron crates for the crockery manufacturers – which I think could be done to advantage.

I forgot to say that Rotherwood is still to the fore, and appears a fine healthy forest. This is one of Scott's Kenilworth scenes.[53]

The ride from Sheffield to Derby is through a lovely country, particularly as you approach Derby. But from Derby to Birmingham 'tis rather tame. There is an interesting view of the old village of Tamworth, with its venerable church and old castle.

CHAPTER 14

Birmingham

Regarding Birmingham I scarcely know what to say, for I have grown so intimate with its every street, lane, and building, that they appear old acquaintances. The situation is good in many ways; high and elevated, it is healthful, and is the center and highway of all thoroughfares throughout England.

The artisans of this town are decidedly superior to Sheffield. No combinations are here permitted to affect trade. Lively competition gives a healthy tone to all transactions, and the result is that the trade of the town is steadily increasing, all are in comfortable circumstances, and general contentment and happiness seems to be the lot of the good folks of Birmingham.

Many of the manufactories are worth visiting. Among the most interesting are the:

Glass Works of Chance Bros. & Co.[54]

Glass Bottles, etc. of (I forget)
Electro Plating
Gun Barrel & Sword Manufacturing
Gun proving Proof house
Wood Screw Making

There are several very fine show rooms also, but 'twould be endless work to note their contents. The most beautiful is the Papier Mache Room, where you see the chairs at 20 pounds each, and everything else in proportion.

The Plated Ware and Bronze Rooms are also very fine. The Medal Manufacture is very clever, and the cutting of the die is a most laborious and minute job; it has to be done with a strong magnifying glass and is a very expensive matter.

There are some good churches in the town, but none of much interest. The Polytechnic Institution has a good suite of rooms.[55] King Edward's School is a superb building by Barry - it is esteemed his masterpiece - and many boys are taught here.[56] Prince Albert was much struck with the order and government of the boys; as he and the Queen entered, the little fellows - some hundred in number - were instructed previously to make a bow to Her Majesty and stand. They did so, and did more, for to the astonishment of their teacher their loyalty became so ungovernable at the presence of their dear Queen, that simultaneously they all roared out, "God save the Queen!" As she was leaving, the building almost trembled with their deafening cheer - true honest, English hearts in these brave lads; they showed their manly independence yet sincere love and loyalty in their spontaneous expression in the presence of Her Majesty.

The Town Hall is a very famous building. It is an exact copy of the Temple of Jupiter that formerly existed in Athens. Its size is 152 feet in length, 65 feet in height, and 65 feet in width, which is considered the perfection of building proportions.[57]

I had the pleasure of attending a concert of vocal and instrumental music in this hall. The instruments numbered about one hundred and the vocalists the same. When all united in the sacred chorus, 'twas grand. The hall is admirable for its sound: a single voice fills it easily and not the slightest echo appears.

The organ in this Town Hall is the largest, sweetest, and most powerful of the many I have heard in England; its size is enormous – height 50 feet, width 40 feet, depth 15 feet; upwards of 4,000 pipes, the largest 3 x 35 feet; with a chime of 40 bells; and having about 75 stops. Such is the power of this organ that when its full power is brought out, the effect is felt by passers-by on the other side of the street, by the trembling of the earth.[58]

Some time ago, a celebrated German player was here, and in his ecstasy at the eloquence of music which he was producing, he forgot all but the occasion, threw his German soul of music totally into the action of the moment – and such was the delight of the audience that they all stood up simultaneously; and while in this attitude of deepest attention, the trumpet sounded with such a force as to shake the massive building to its foundation, so much so as to terrify the audience; but like the charming of the snake – which you know will take your life as payment for its melody – this fine musician, with the noble instrument held the audience so completely fascinated, that they would rather have been crushed to death than lose one note of the sublime and soul-stirring music which he poured upon their delighted ears. And when he ceased, many screamed and fainted from over-wrought feeling. What a tribute of applause this same suffering must have been to the musician. It is a fine proof of the distinction between mechanical music, and music of the soul, when poured out with artistical skill.

I heard this organ myself, but by a less skillful player, and yet 'twas thrilling, 'twas sublime; when he opened with clear sweet sounds, you felt how beautiful, then as he melted away into an inaudible whisper, you followed it till you forgot yourself – until awakened by a sound like very thunder, mingled with the melodious shout of a thousand angels; anon the sounds change, one moment you are lifted to the skies, the next you are at the feet of your Creator; finally the music assumes the call for mercy, mingled with praise and thanksgiving. A religious awe comes over you; you feel in the presence of your God – your heart is filled. While in this state the death dirge is played upon the bells and, in the delight of the moment, you have conquered death and are ready to exclaim, "O Death where is thy sting, O Grave where is thy victory!"[59]

Such was the effect of this fine instrument upon me, and such would it be with anyone possessed of a religious feeling, and having a soul for music. Such a hall and organ devoted to musical purposes does great credit to the people of Birmingham. It adorns their labors and proves to the world that while they stand high as one of the great workshops of this country, they are capable of higher and more elevated deeds and enjoyments than their daily occupation would seem to imply.

It is a very interesting country from Birmingham to Wolverhampton – a distance of fifteen miles. Vegetation there is none; the road is like a chain of towns, for every two or three miles you pass through a village of five or six thousand inhabitants, between, around, and behind which are hundreds of coal and iron pits, blasting, smelting, and rolling furnaces, and mills. The whole surface of the country is covered with coal on fire being converted to coke, iron stone being calcined – all so black and dreary that one shudders to look at it. At night, as you ride through this country, it is fearful; every furnace pours forth its blaze; the thousands of coke piles indicate their whereabouts by columns of white smoke with a flame in the center; around the mouth of every shaft and pit are a dozen coal fires in grates, to guard against persons falling in – and through and among all these you perceive hundreds of beings whom you take for men or devils, dancing from one fire to another as if in demon play, although they are in fact tending their fires.

Seated on the top of the coach as you pass through from Birmingham to Wolverhampton, however dark the night elsewhere, here it is always light, and it would be no great task to read a newspaper as the coach proceeds.

A story is told of a poor wight who got riotously drunk, and while in that state of deep sleep he was carried to the heart of the iron region. By and by he awoke and found numbers of black demons dancing around him and the fires; the poor fellow thought he had got to the other world, so when they asked him what trade he belonged to, he answered, "In the other world I was an Excise man, but here I will be anything you like."

CHAPTER 15

Gloucester and Bristol

We must now leave Birmingham and proceed to Gloucester. 'Tis a very old town, and has a noble cathedral which boasts a tower of peculiar beauty and imposing grandeur. I was much pleased with the tombs and monuments here. Besides many ancient ones there was a modern one which attracted much of my attention; 'twas erected by a husband to his wife who was so devoted to him that she preferred braving the deep and the climate of India beside her husband, to remaining in England. In addition to the strong affection to her husband, she possessed equal maternal fondness, for her child was likely to die unless removed to England. And now, faithful to her trust, she leaves her husband whom she had braved so much for, and again she is on the deep. But alas! For the noble mother, she and her child go down in the ship which was never more heard of – and this tomb of purest marble is to record the fidelity, virtue, and noble daring of one of God's best creatures. The design is in keeping – the foreground is the raging sea, angels hover above, and out of the sea rises the mother and her child, with the motto below: "The sea shall give up its dead."[60]

From the cathedral to the ruins of the abbey – nearly a mile – there is a subterranean passage, which none nowadays dares venture into. Many of the houses look very old, but in the vicinity of the spa the town is entirely modern and rather pretty. A very small piece of the old wall remains. I stopped at the Bell Tavern, a very old house in which George Whitefield, the preacher, and a Bishop of Gloucester, were born.[61] After spending a Sunday in the town, I proceeded onward, towards Bristol. Cheltenham, about seven miles from Gloucester, towards Birmingham, is a very handsome modern town, and a very fashionable watering place.

The country from Gloucester to Bristol is of the most varied and magnificent character. You have Wales to the right, rising gradually from the valley of the Severn, until you lose its distant top in the mist – all highly cultivated; green is the verdure as if it were summer; the fences of hedges, the trees, the noblemen's mansions, or the rural cottages, the Severn itself, the immense bottom land of the Severn with its tower here and there, and the towering spire of the church rising from among houses and trees, asserting at once the devotion of the people, and its high title over the chapels of the dissenters; and, if to perfect the picture, you see the tower of Gloucester Cathedral from all the country around, properly situated to overlook its children, the parish churches. A more lovely country cannot be found in England.

Bristol. This is a city built by the Romans. It is at once ancient and modern. I stopped one night in a hotel called the White Lion, which has been a hotel for 500 years. The modern city, being by far the greater in proportion, is very pretty and admirably built; while Clifton, which is merely a continuation of the city in a certain direction, is actually beautiful and picturesque. On the summit of Clifton there is the best camera obscura[62] I have ever seen – for twenty miles around it shows you the minutest objects in general scenery; and the winding of the river is beautiful. The inhabitants are very good-looking people.

I understand that in a population of 100,000, there is an excess of 7,000 females over the males. Memo: a good place for a bachelor to fish for a wife.

The kindness of the McDowells, who made me become their guest for nearly a week, made my visit to Bristol delightful – and it will never be in my lot to meet greater or more disinterested kindness.

To get to jotting on London, I skip noting some beautiful scenes between Bristol and London.

CHAPTER 16

London

M arch 2, 1844. London! What music there is in the name! How am I to express my first impressions of thy greatness! My first ramble was through Green Park and St. James Park, surrounded by palaces. 'Twas Sunday, I roamed on, noticing the tame ducks and swans, fed by the people, in the pond; passed through the Horse Guards; observed the well-formed guardsmen with their white leather breeches, red coats, and white plumes on brass caps, as they sat sentry on their black chargers.

I continued on to Westminster in all its ancient grandeur; thence to the new Parliament Houses,[63] and Westminster Bridge; thence down the Strand; passed the Temple Bar; came upon St. Paul's, a gorgeous pile; pushing forward I came to the Post Office, Bank, Mansion House,[64] Guild Hall,[65] and London Bridge; and after attending Divine Service in St. Paul's, I returned to the Gloucester Hotel to dine, having walked ten miles, besides attending worship, between an 11 o'clock breakfast and an 8 o'clock dinner.

And what are my first impressions? That there can be only one London. That this one London is the finest of cities – 'tis a city of palaces, with the widest and cleanest of streets, loveliest of parks, and the quietest, best behaved and strictest town I ever visited. 'Twas delightful to see the inhabitants, in hundreds and thousands, crowd the parks to enjoy the fresh breeze on this Sunday afternoons: so happy, well dressed, and politely independent they looked. I gazed upon them as the descendants of those stout-hearted citizens of London who maintained their honor and independence so well in the feudal ages gone by. The same middle-statured, square-shouldered, and rubicund-faced people I fancied to exist a long time ago - and here they are still rebuilding their town, making

(gap in manuscript)

I set to observing the inmates, the attraction became equally as powerful as the preceding, and again I was charmed. 'Twas hard to tell which most to admire, therefore I deem both worthy of admiration beyond all praise.

In the splendid mansions, showing architectural skill and taste, in the elegant internal embellishment and furniture; in the paintings and in the statuary; various articles of virtu; in the horses and carriages; in the taste and splendor of entertainment and hospitality; in the manners which are continually refined and refining; in the high-toned honor and code of honor which is established and strictly guarded; in all these I see the advantages of an aristocracy in a free country. They are the modelers of taste, refiners of manners, cultivators and patrons of the arts, in short, they are the conservation of all that is delightful, elevating, and refining to mankind; they are a model school for all to copy; and, although socially the commoners of England cannot meet them in their inner circle, yet their pleasure, elevation, and happiness is much enhanced and refined by seeing and copying the ancient and high-born aristocracy of England – and all this is done without any overbearing spirit on the one hand, or servility on the other. And the rank of nobility and aristocracy to superior wealth and intellectual greatness.

There is a great number of omnibuses running from one extremity of the town to the other, through cross street and byways - making the probable distance for each omnibus about five miles from the Bank, from which point they all start. You can ride the whole five miles for sixpence, or less at the same charge. They go at a great speed and make only momentary stoppages - performing the five miles in a little over the half hour. Sometimes a street will be so crowded that a stop is indispensable, but soon the hundreds of vehicles melt away from the jam, each its own way - it is astonishing to see the drivers wend through among carts, carriages, and all sorts of conveyances zig-zag! No clear straight line of driving in the chief thoroughfares - for you meet at least thirty vehicles a minute, room for all which you must make, while others you have got to pass, keeping the mind on the fret in expectation of a smash, which seems never to occur. And it is a wonder to gentlemen well-acquainted with the streets of London, how such a mass of carriages and human beings continually moving, do not fall foul of each other and produce accidents - but they never occur.

Speaking with a friend, I observed how odd it was that the Bank of England should be the center from which the omnibuses should hail. "Ah!" he remarked, "There is more than omnibuses here. The Bank of England is the center of the whole world; not an act takes place in the Bank Chamber which does not affect the remotest point of civilization." And in the broad sense, I am inclined to think there is some truth to it.

The streets of London are wide, smooth, and clean. The wooden pavement is being laid down instead of the stone, all over the city; and in a few years there will be nothing but wooden streets. And all the streets which are wide have been made so in the last fifty years, hence they are all lined with beautiful houses and shops. Everything indicates an extended idea in taste - ceilings high, windows large, shops wide - and, indeed, everything on the most comprehensive scale.

The West End, which means all that part of London west of Temple Bar, where London proper begins,[66] covers a space of ground about four miles in length by as many in width, the great portion of this being covered with the mansions of the nobility and gentry, the palaces of majesty and the parks - is perhaps the most magnificent city of which the world could ever boast - not excepting those ancient cities of which we have such beautiful drawings extant.

The Tower is a very interesting structure from the varied scenes of which it has been author.[67] Its history is the history of England. As a building, there is nothing captivating about it. It covers many acres of ground and is ancient and old-fashioned in its arches, gates, corridors, etc. It is much visited on account of the armory of ancient arms and coats of mail - which is exposed in fine order. To show the coats of mail to advantage, the exact likeness of the horse and King represented, is made of wood - full-size - and both covered with the very last mail fought in. Many of these coats of mail are inlaid with gold, and very valuable. There are many soldiers on foot also, and the effect is such, that when one enters the room, the imagination almost pictures the statues alive. By a beautiful arrangement of gun barrels, locks, stocks, pistols, ramrods, and bayonets - many flowers are represented around the walls and on the ceiling, as the rose, passion flower, etc. Queen Elizabeth is among the equestrian statues, in the dress which she wore on going to Parliament after the victory over the Spanish Armada, the page is leading the horse - the whole looking much like life.

In another part of the Tower is the room where the crown jewels are kept, constantly guarded by soldiers. The crown of the present Queen is most beautiful. The whole contents of the room could be packed in a hogshead - aye, in half a hogshead - and yet the value is three million sterling, which is equal to fifteen millions of dollars. Among the articles I was struck with was a sword called the Sword of Mercy, another the Sword of Justice, another the Sword of the Defender of the Faith – the instruments of royalty.

In a stroll I visited Tattersall's, celebrated as the great auction mart for horses; Mark Lane, the great corn market;[68] Smithfield, the great cattle market; the Hungerford market for meat, fish, and vegetables; Doctors' Commons,[69] where so many wills have been buried, and passing on I visited the Herald Office[70] where escutcheons and coats of arms are preserved and manufactured for those who have none. The Serjeants' Inn – Lincoln's Inn - places of law.[71] Vice Chancellor Knight-Bruce's Court and Vice Chancellor Wigram's Court,[72] and the Court of Rolls,[73] listening to some musty speeches in each, for I observed that in one feature they were all alike, videlicet, the prosy laziness of the speaker, and the indifference of the judge to what was said.

The O'Connell Dinner, Covent Garden Theater, March 12.[74]

Twelve hundred sat down to dinner, of which I was one. As many ladies filled the boxes of the theater as spectators. 'Twas an interesting sight to see so many well-dressed and intelligent people congregate to signify their approbation of a political movement in favor of suffering humanity. Whether right or wrong they meant honestly – although I decidedly differ with them.

O'Connell was received with great warmth; the ladies waved their handkerchiefs and the gentlemen their table napkins – overhead, making the vast area look like a waving field of (what shall I say) Indian corn.

The dinner was cold and was cooked three miles from where it was eaten, but that is nothing in London. Every guest had a napkin and finger glasses[75] were handed around afterwards: 1,200 table napkins!

The music was tolerable only, for London – but the speeches admirable. Mr. Duncombe,[76] who was in the Chair, made a very appropriate speech and concluded by proposing the Queen, Prince Albert, and

Royal Family, Army and Navy – and finally the great gun of the evening, Daniel O'Connell, the father of his country. Long and loud were the cheers. To this toast we were told to fill a bumper and no daylight. This drew out Mr. O'Connell, a heavy-made, square-countenanced, and bad-looking personage. While the wig shaded his face to his disadvantage, it did not much alter his general expression. Silent – a vulgar looking man, but when animated by his own eloquence or the subject, he looked a noble being, every lineament of his countenance beaming with love for his race, or with lofty and withering scorn for his supposed or real oppressors. I understand that to hear him once you hear him always – that is, that his style becomes irksome – but to my ear and apprehension he is a most powerful speaker. His countenance changes with the spirit of every sentence; one moment, when speaking of the love and veneration of Ireland toward him, his face was actually that of a higher being than man – 'twas childish loveliness in simplicity and expression. Again when he spoke of the English tribute now being paid him, pride, gratitude, and love were all visible and yet beautifully mingled in his face and bearing – and yet, when his subject drew him that way, he could look the very savage, next the good-natured clown, and finally a clear, earnest, and intelligent man, in the summing up of his subject - often deviating but always coming back to his points.

The Earl of Shrewsbury next spoke.[77] A very different-looking person to O'Connell. He spoke feelingly of the condition of Ireland, and called O'Connell the father of his country. The Earl, in a suit of black buttoned up to the chin, spoke well and prettily – the result of a finished education, of a fair intellect. When he ceased speaking, I retired, leaving the party in full enjoyment. I am delighted with public meetings here. No foolish ass is allowed to speak, and eloquent and intelligent men are so numerous, that it is difficult to tell when you have heard the best, while you must pronounce all good. No speaker here ever appeals to aught but the common sense of the people. No one dares to rouse their prejudices or play upon their fancy and imagination. Nor do they dare to flatter their hearers with self-love. How delightful this is – that you can listen to varied eloquence on all subjects, without hearing it degraded by pandering to man's bad passions or to his ignorance - it indicates a high state of civilization. A touch of this is O'Connell's fault, but his Irish blarney clothes a thing that in broad English would be naked and deformed. My impression of O'Connell on the finish of his speech was, that he was a deep Jesuit, who would assume any character to mask his wishes, and who is evidently deeply bent on gaining an ascendancy for the Romish Church at the expense of destroying the Episcopal Protestant Church - he won't succeed.

Jullien's Masked Ball, Covent Garden Theater.[78]

This was a showy affair. The pit of the theater was covered over, making a dancing floor for about two thousand people, which number was in attendance besides about two thousand more in the boxes as spectators. Indeed, there was not an empty seat in the boxes and gallery, or an uncovered spot on the floor of the house.

The dancers were in all kinds of costumes - Turks, Hunters, Highlanders, Devils, Sailors, etc. The ladies were equally varied in their dress, and all wore masks. By paying 10/6 for a ticket and 4/6 for a mask, I reached the dancing floor without doffing either coat or cap, nor did I put on my mask - having no fear of being recognized in this city, for I never knew a place where an honest man could be so safe from recognition as in this same London. A thief is not quite so safe for the policeman will make his acquaintance under all circumstances.

But to return; the place was hung with crimson and white drapery all around and the ceiling so likewise; besides the usual gas lamps of glass, each containing a hundred lights, there were many oil hanging lamps for the occasion - making this room as brilliant as day. The music from a hundred instruments was excellent. The pillars of this hall were wreathed with artificial flowers of various hues; and when the dancers moved in the graceful waltz or quadrille, the scene was quite enchanting. Four thousand people in full dress in an elegantly adorned and well-lighted room must always be an uncommon and delightful sight. It was so to me on this occasion. Although I did not join in the dance, I was soon in lively chat with many a gay and well-made masked beauty. True, they had the advantage of me - they being masked while I was not - I cared not. Whenever I saw what I thought likely to be a pretty girl I at once struck up an acquaintance, which never lasted over three minutes, so that during the two hours I remained, I probably conversed with perhaps thirty or forty lovely women. But alas for the poetry of the thing - I soon found that there was not a virtuous woman on the floor. And, latterly, when they began to cast aside their masks, I was amazed at the exceeding beauty of many of these girls. One girl was there of surpassing loveliness, and in her face was depicted refinement, education, modesty, and pride; her eye brilliant and honest and her figure and bearing actually majestic. And yet that poor girl was degraded forever - cast out from the society of the good - perhaps by means of a villainous deceiver of our sex. She, a creature of surpassing loveliness and grace, must submit to the rude brutality of the midnight rake and drunkard, and finally pay the debt of abused nature in an early grave.

If a man commits murder he suffers death! If he forges or steals he is banished from his country for life - but if he steals the happiness of a woman's whole life here, and endangers her salvation hereafter, it is accounted nothing; he stalks in society as if he were an honest man, and yet it is a heinous and terrible sin in comparison with theft, forgery, or even murder. If there is justice in God's laws, 'twill not be the poor girl who will be worst punished - he that so awfully sinned in compelling her to sin, must account to his Creator for much of the sin of her life.

No educated and thinking man who has seen the world in all its phases and forms, but must be filled with loathing disgust towards those poor creatures who are to be bought to gratify man's wicked lust.

I hope to have arrived at that period of life at which we view affairs with reflection, and I am firmly settled in my own mind that the man who seduces a poor girl, be she rich or poor, ugly or beautiful, is a villain, cold-hearted and dishonest, who would steal if there was no danger of punishment – aye, and murder, too, in the dark, if his own filthy body was sure to be safe.

I am not so silly as to believe, that in the present artificial state of society all women can be preserved from degradation, Alas! Poverty prostrates many and natural wickedness some more; and this class in society will continue to exist as long as the ignorant depravity of man's nature demands it. But when, in this class, you see a pretty and interesting girl, who would have made a good wife and kind mother perhaps, ask her why she fell, why she forgot herself, and she will answer, "Sir, I was seduced by one whom I loved." And yet, such is the thoughtlessness of many a good man, that few will believe such an assertion from a poor fallen girl – but this is part of her punishment.

All my life I have held women in high esteem, I love to think them purer, holier, and more affectionate than men. I have found them so always – kind, honest, and obliging. And can I then refrain from feeling for this unfortunate branch of the family of women. Oh! No! True, many are degraded that you can no longer recognize a single trait of woman – all has become brutal. This is terrible, really terrible, but there are many not yet below the compass of your compassion. I frequently meet such on the streets here, neatly dressed and bold in their approach; but when I speak mildly to them (and they see I am not likely to visit their house) and address them as if I recognized a fellow creature in them – oh, how quickly the sensitive nature of woman tells them they have met a friend; how quick their boldness sinks into timidity; how proud they are if you allow them to talk a bit with you, and with what politeness and sorrow they bid goodbye – perhaps to meet a brute. Poor girls, I feel for them, and I pay part of my debt to virtuous women in feeling for the unfortunate of their sex, when they dare not stoop to save or lift them up.

And so the gay and brilliant ball, instead of producing pleasant impressions on me, filled me with sad thoughts penned on the foregoing pages. All the women in this room were of what are called the better class of prostitutes. They danced well, waltzed well, conversed correctly and many in educated style. The great proportion were young and beautiful - all God's creatures, reduced by man's ungoverned passion to the level of the brute race.

A couple of hours made me wearied of the scene - I wended my way towards my hotel, a sadder if not a wiser man.

Drury Lane.[79] Venerable house - you have been the theater of many fine spirits, Sheridan, Kean, Kemble, etc., all are your children.[80] In you Shakespeare has been embalmed, ever young, ever brilliant. On your boards thousands of eyes have been riveted, night after night for many a day - listening to an exposition of human nature, clothed in rare eloquence, deep pathos, pure and elevated feeling, soul-stirring wit, and in richly adorned truth - but, Old Drury, your day of change has come. No longer does the legitimate drama please the public taste, nor does the same noble mind besport on your boards - but instead thereof, a paltry Italian opera and French ballet are the only things which now fill your boxes, pit, and purse. And with these foreign pastimes you have established bad habits. Your noble salon, fit for Princes to tread, surely was designed for different purposes, than it is now applied to. Well may parents fear to trust their sons within your walls, for there they will always find sin and destruction decked in most charming colors. Aye, within your walls they will meet the rarest beauty covering deep degradation and death.

The British Museum - supposed to be the largest in the world - is well worthy of a long visit.[81] The Elgin marbles, ancient antiquities, mummies, sculptures, birds, beasts, reptiles, insects, fish, geological specimens, all are complete as embracing everything known in the world. The library is immense also. It is a pleasing trait in the government to allow such an establishment to be free to all. It is open three days each week and many thousands weekly throng to visit it. The original Magna Carta is a great curiosity. The Elgin marbles illustrate the beautiful, artistical taste of the ancient Greeks; and the stone coffins and sculpture of the Egyptians prove that with all our boasted wisdom we're in many things unequal to our forefathers.

'Twere vain to attempt a minute record of the institution. Every specimen is the best of its kind, and the number almost endless.

Westminster Abbey![82] You have only to place yourself within the walls of this noble and ancient place of worship, to feel conclusively your own nothingness in this world; for around you on every side you perceive the tombs and monuments of Kings who made the earth tremble for very terror; Queens who were at once brilliant, cruel, and wicked; Queens who were legally murdered and the murderer Queen in one common resting place;[83] Bishops and Priests who held the conscience of the world in bondage; Knights who would have faced an army undaunted; Admirals who established in England's sway over all the world; statesmen who ennobled themselves in wielding successfully for a period the destinies of this country and her tributaries; historians who recorded them all and their doings for our benefit, and poets, who embellished and beautified all.

Strange are the sensations which a visit to the place produces. Wonderfully is the magic power of printing here felt; it makes us intimate with the dead – the past; the Edwards, the Henrys, Queen Elizabeth, Mary, and Mary of Scots; the Jameses, the Charleses, the Georges - all seem like known acquaintances. Your mind rapidly surveys the actions of their reigns as you approach and hang over their tombs; you blame them for this, you exalt them for that; distance weakens their bad acts and illumines the good, and kind charity throws a friendly and farewell glance over every tomb. Poor Mary of Scots! I have been in her bedroom and touched her bed in her Northern Palace; I have been in her English prison, and now I have seen her tomb, and I know not why, but a painful sorrow oppresses me at every evidence of the poor Queenly girl whose surpassing beauty was equaled only by the kindness of her nature. Peace to her name. Yes, a visit to this common resting place of the illustrious dead is a wholesale lesson – recollect the fine minds whose meditations had only to be expressed to become law to mankind - Kings and Queens on whose sway the sun never set. Think of these, and see them now cold, inanimate dust; while they lived their greatness was felt and acknowledged, but now they are forgotten, like the storm of yesterday, and the world wages on quite as well without them.

This is our common fate - and yet, poor silly creatures, we fight and bicker, emulate and envy, self-exalt ourselves and condemn others, as if we had no long lesson - some thousand years long - telling us of the absurdity of such conduct. Strange fallacy! We study such lessons, we feel their truth, and after conning them over, we return to the world to repeat our follies anew.

I have heard it said that some men believe in a previous existence and that such, when they have for the first time visited a strange place, if struck with an idea of faint recollection of previous acquaintance with such place, having accounted for it by supposing that their spirit, while embodied in a previous being, had lived here, and now tells the fact to the understanding. However farfetched such an idea, yet history engenders such a feeling on visiting Westminster Abbey. You look around you, and though your first visit, you know all, your imagination helps your recollection, and you see their acts pass before you as they occurred a long time ago.

The Abbey as a building is very grand, its towers are rich and imposing - inside, it is one series of columns and arches, the stone roof exquisitely carved and gilded, and the great height of the ceiling, make it altogether a solemn, Gothic pile - doing great credit to its builders - as a fitting place of worship of that God who deserves eternal thanksgiving.

The tombs and monuments are the chief object of attraction. Many of them are gorgeous, one of the best that of Mary Queen of Scots. 'Tis a royal canopy surmounted by a crown - under and in which is the tomb of stone in which the beautiful Queen is laid in marble sculpture - an exact likeness - while within her dust reposes.

The abbey is crowded with monuments and tombs, all of exquisite workmanship and all recording the illustrious and departed great.

Here the Queens and Kings have been crowned and in the same chair for many hundred years - and in one of these chairs is the crowning stone of Scotland placed.[84]

Bazaars of London are pretty places - that in Oxford Street is the most pleasing; this is an omnium gatherum embracing toys to paintings. 'Tis strange to see a hundred female shopkeepers under one roof, all independent of each other, attending their matters with a quietness that seemed delightful. There are few pleasanter places for an hour's lounge than these same bazaars. Many ladies think so and that makes it more agreeable for poor fellows in single blessedness.

The National Gallery[85] is another of these government institutions where admittance is free. Many of the finest paintings by West, Reynolds, etc. are there. No paintings except the very best are allowed - hence, though few in number, the specimens are beautiful.

To continue a description of all the places I visited in London would require much time, and as I am now on shipboard and on the ocean, steering westward, I find my mind loath to go over the scenes. Suffice it to say that after visiting the Opera, public buildings, and several public meetings, I grew tired of London and hurried down to Scotland to say adieu to my northern friends. And kindly did they testify their welcome, for not content with domestic hospitality, they honored me with a public manifestation of their goodness - inasmuch as the leading inhabitants of the old town of Stranraer gave me a public dinner - as they kindly said - in testimony of their high regard for myself and my mother's son. As usual on such occasions I made a speech and, odd to think, was neither elevated nor abashed by the whole affair. This was not required to tell me how much of my countrymen's esteem I enjoyed, and yet, 'twas agreeable - because, when I recollect that I am most likely transplanted for life to a new land, it is delightful to think that those whom I deserted regret my departure, and exult in my advancing fortunes.

How lasting are the ties of youth? As I roamed or rode through all the old haunts of my boyhood, I saw in the moldering fences and paltry rivulets nothing but beauty; the cottagers' faces, as they smiled their God's blessing on me, beamed with high intelligence in my fancy; the old women as they hirped along, seemed possessed of some charm which cloaked or counterbalanced their deformity – in short, the place and people were colored in the utmost loveliness in my imagination; my whole past existence passed and repassed rapidly before me; pictured in harmonious youth and loveliness, which seemed to be renewed in this visit. Scenery, climate, people – all, all as I used to know them. But how few, of those I now said goodbye to will I ever see again. Since my last visit, many have gone to another world; ere I again return many will have followed; and ten or fifteen years hence, my native spot will be a foreign land to me. And yet, 'tis as nature dictates and it should be so. Were we to live forever or did we continually feel that our intercourse here below must be short with each other – would there exist those friendships which tie man to man? Oh, no! And it is well that even those we love should pass away, for they go to a better world, and we, by their loss, are taught that we must soon follow. This gives the romantic to life; it subdues our natures as music tames the savage beast, and teaches us to enjoy with trembling.

And must I bid adieu to the Old Scotland again! And yet, 'tis so; and to thee Old England, and as I say farewell let me pray 'tis not forever – for though I am content with the land of my adoption, yet I can never cease to love thee. Since I touched thy shores some four months ago, I have met nothing but kindness, and that so unbounded as to cause me often to pause and ask what it all meant, why I am lionized, waited upon, and overwhelmed with distinguished hospitality by Englishmen. Truly and clearly do I know 'tis from no greatness in me, from no advantage I can grant in return. In short, I am fully persuaded all arises from natural kindness and frankness of character and that any other visitor, properly introduced, would meet exactly the same attention. And what noble trait is this in Englishmen – 'twould cover a thousand sins and faults. Britain, I owe thee a great debt! For this visit has taught me how highly you appreciate honesty and honor and taught me the vital consequence of losing these – for in losing these thy doors would be closed forever, which are now so temptingly open to thy deserving friends. As I approached thy rock-bound and mist-enveloped shores, I knew what was enshrined behind. As now I leave, the same cloak of mist divides us, and for many a day I see thee no more.

CHAPTER 17

Steam Ship to America

O n the ocean wave: with our faces to the setting sun, in the good ship Acadia.[86] We steam along bravely; if the wind blows fair, very well, if not we will go forward in spite of it. And if a kind Providence will smile on us, we will soon be in America. Passengers count ninety-four. And while I am not in the least sea sick, I have a roommate very sick, a lubberly fellow who never leaves his bed and is likely to be sick all the voyage. So much are my vexations. Whatever bad impression I have had against the steam ships I now withdraw – for, although crowded, still there is comfort, delightful food and plenty of it, good wines and excellent attention on part of stewards and waiters – and for so short a voyage what more can a single man require. And as to the capability of the ship for fighting the elements – I think the Acadia perfect. She skims the waves as quietly and softly as if it were on a placid lake, pushing herself onward, without any evident struggle. We have not experienced a gale yet, but from what she has already done, I feel safe in her qualifications for any and all weathers.

We are now eight days out and have experienced strong head winds ever since we left Liverpool. This will make our passage a long one. The time is spent in reading till lunch, cards till dinner, reading till tea time, and cards again afterwards.

Among the passengers the Canadians are the most numerous, but we have, besides, Swiss, English, Americans, Germans, Spaniards, French, Irish, and Scotch.

There is some heavy gambling going on, occasionally a warm dispute, and constantly a very great noise, very much to the annoyance of some and delight of others. Our lady passengers - some six in number, are so uninviting and so well taken care of, that I have so far avoided an acquaintance with any of them.

My voyage eastward was made under an experienced captain, always attentive to his duty, and if sometimes gruff, yet always sensible. This voyage westward is under a shallow-headed commander, who is trying to play the superb in the drawing room, making many feel offended; and instead of attending to his ship, plays cards from morning till midnight - and for heavy stakes, too. God grant us a safe passage to Boston, with the protection of a good Providence; I hope to get over in safety, and it will be my care to keep from under the same person's command (Captain Ryrie)[87] hereafter.

CHAPTER 18

Additional Comments

Having a few leaves to spare and some leisure on shipboard, I refer to my notebook for some subjects worth retaining recollection of, and now proceed to jot them.

In my journey through England and Scotland, I visited many places which are not noticed in these pages, but some are too important to overlook as long as a few pages of this book remain.

The noblemen of England are very kind in allowing all strangers to visit their mansions, and keep servants expressly to show the premises to such strange visitors. The government is now following their example by making the public institutions free of admission. This liberality must tend to improve the taste of the people and give a thirst for further information.

One of the everyday things of England are the chimes of bells, much sweeter than the tolling bells, and when on a Sunday morning you hear a whole city filled with the sound of music of a hundred chimes, it might be compared to the minstrelsy of a crowd of angels telling the citizens 'tis God's holy day and bidding them go forth to worship.

The spires of England are also an everyday spectacle. Ride through what county you may, you will see in the distance the beautiful spire of the village parish church; all old churches built by our forefathers as citadels of that Church for which they fought and which they hoped to see perpetuated in their children for many generations to come.

The cathedrals and churches of England are one of her brightest ornaments – all old, finely built, with stained windows, sculptured walls, and Gothic architecture – they are different from modern buildings, and are in a fine state of preservation generally, and have been hallowed as places of worship for so many generations that one looks upon them with affection and holy awe.

As the Cathedral of York is the finest cathedral, so the Church of Saint Mary Redcliffe, in Bristol, is the finest of churches.[88] Indeed, I consider this church superior to the Bristol Cathedral. If I recollect right, William Penn and his family are buried in this church, and his Indian trophies are hung up on the rafters of the church.[89] On my visit to this church, I was accompanied by a beautiful warm-hearted girl, and our names are duly recorded together in the church books as a future evidence against us.

The abbey at Bath is very pretty and full of monuments, among which I noticed many names known to the world at large; also many Scotchmen, poets, soldiers, naval men, statesmen, and others.

Bath is a beautiful town; high and steep hills surround it; its crescents, streets, houses, shops, and parks are beautiful and tasteful, its ball rooms and watering rooms chaste and beautiful.

Railroads in England strike the traveler with astonishment: miles above miles of tunnels, in some places one tunnel from three to five miles; valleys arched over by hundreds of arches, hundreds of feet in depth; stations built to contain the commerce of the whole world; buildings vying in beauty and architectural taste with the most noble mansions; necessary conveniences for travelers so commodious, plentiful, and admirably arranged that there is nothing to wish for; the great retinue of the servants at every station; their extreme civility to assist and wait upon your baggage, and their being forbidden to make fees is most delightful; the superb cars you ride in; the great steady speed, the ease of motion – tend to make railway traveling a great pleasure, without room for a single grumble or complaint.

I had collected notes for a valuable chapter on railroads, but have lost them and forgot the subject, which I must regret, as it would have been valuable as a practical view in America.

Friends and Neighbors

Laing Family

Mrs. Laing, Matron, Gillespie's Hospital, Edinburgh.[90] I found her to be a nice-looking old maid of about fifty years, fresh in face, rosy in cheeks, lively and artless in conversation; small in stature; delighted to see me, as I was to see her; possessing an affectionate recollection of my mother – and is charmed with the idea of renewing that friendship and correspondence with me which she so faithfully kept up with my mother for thirty years – although they never saw each other.

Hannay Family

Mrs. Hannay, Stranraer, is now an old lady, lively and gay, and as full of conversation as ever – but, although no difference is perceptible for the past five years, yet she must be near her end. When she goes, one of my worldly links – aye, a link of the finest and most refined texture, will be broken in my chain of friends.

Miss Grace Hannay bids fair to be an old maid. She is looking well and is the same rattling, trolloping, singing, praying girl I have always known her to be.

Walter Hannay – London - An amiable warm-hearted fellow, too easy for this world, devotes his time to painting and hopes to arrive at some eminence ultimately. 19 Arundel Street, Strand.

McMaster Family
Mrs. McMaster is a beautiful woman, in delicate health – her children are overgrown, clumsy, dullish children. Her husband is a lazy, indolent, simple creature – unfit to take care of himself, to say nothing of his family.

Lambs Family
Rev. Mr. Lambs' family, Kirkmaiden, Wigtownshire, Scotland.

Mr. Lambs is a fine, intelligent, but quiet man, just fit for a country parish, and unqualified for the turmoil of a more active sphere.

Mrs. Lambs is as young looking as ever; she makes a good wife, affectionate mother, and is a warm friend.

Marion, the senior daughter, is a blooming girl, possessed of good, natural abilities, with an excellent country education. It is lamentable that her parents' income won't permit her being sent to England for two years; it would refine her in mind, body, taste, and manners, and make her a superior woman. I fear circumstances doom her to the poor country situation.

James is at present a soft looking lad, but his aunts say that he has more in him than appears.

Agnes, Annie, and Patrick are good-looking children.

McDowell Family

Robert McDowell and family, Bristol.

He is a Scotchman, who has accumulated a snug sum in England. He is in appearance very like a person whom I knew by the nickname of Cheeks – but in all other respects a superior man, being a self-made, good-natured, sensible, modest, and money-making man.

Mrs. McDowell is a nice, good-looking Englishwoman, more polished than her husband – a most amiable lady.

Miss McDowell is a sweet girl, politely educated, and will make a good, affectionate, and sensible wife.

Mary Jane is a nice, affectionate little girl, very beautiful eyes and interesting countenance, promises to shoot up a fine, blooming woman.

Nelly is a nice little girl.

Robert is a fine, handsome lad; although now a child, will make if he lives, a superior man.

APPENDIX A: LETTER TO CONSTITUENTS

W.A. THOMSON, M.P., ON THE POLITICAL SITUATION.

A LETTER TO HIS CONSTITUENTS.

To the People of Welland:

As your representative in the Dominion Parliament, I find it my duty, while it is a pleasure, to give you my thoughts and observations on the events of the hour.

I lately mailed to each voter in the County, irrespective of his political bias, my Drummondville speech. To those who have read it, it must be clear that I am essentially a Liberal in politics: that I have every faith in the people, and am not afraid to entrust the whole national weal in the hands of the whole people. I do not think that the advancement of what is curiously enough called the "masses," will ever be fully carried out except by the masses themselves. There is an unnatural antagonism between "homespun" and "broad cloth." You even see it between town and country. You can prove this, by observing that the rural majorities are generally Liberal, while the town majorities are generally Tory, or what they call Conservative. There are more tailors' shops in town, and the creed of the town is formed on the "goose" basis to a very considerable extent. And, in this case, there is not much difference between a tailor's goose and an ordinary one.[91]

I can easily understand *two* Liberal parties existing in Canada. One, based upon a narrow and contracted process of development: the other, upon a broad and expansive development of systems of industry, education, and public improvement. But what is called Conservatism, and as it has been acted upon, I admit my inability to understand; especially as applied to a country like Canada, where everything has to be done by the people themselves, and where Governments and Parliaments are no way different from the people by tradition or usage, as in old monarchies.

I regard the resignation of the Macdonald Ministry on the fifth day of November, 1873, (this month and year), and the advent of the Liberal party to power, as more than an expression of opinion on the Pacific Scandal.[92] There was partisan prejudice enough in the House to have upheld the Ministry on this subject, bad as it was, and it would have been upheld had there not been an unseen growth of human thought going on for some time past, and pointing clearly against everything smacking of Toryism. This mental condition induced men in and out of Parliament to seize the odious Pacific affair as an excuse to go over to the support of Liberalism.

The unquestionable ability of Sir John A. Macdonald,[93] and the rough vigor and administrative capacity of the late Sir George Cartier,[94] required to be combined to uphold Toryism. Both men were thorough Tories. The one held power in his province through the Church: the other, in Ontario, through his social attractiveness, his intellectual brilliancy, and his parliamentary tact.

With the death of Sir George Cartier, the continuation of the Macdonald Ministry became an impossibility. Before the death of Sir George, he could not be elected for Montreal; the traditional power was already passing away; while in Ontario, as shown at the late elections, notwithstanding the extraordinary elements brought to their aid, the Macdonald Government was left in the minority. Thus, the defeat of the late Ministry not only conveys to the understanding the defeat of a party or principle, but the final obliteration of Toryism for a century to come. And Toryism has held sway more or less for about one hundred years in what is now called Ontario.

In the first days of Confederation the eastern and western provinces found themselves in a state of transition and transformation. The material interests to be conserved and the pecuniary interests to be obtained placed political sentiment in abeyance, and induced the support, for the moment, of whatever Government happened to be in power. But with the final solidification of material interests, political thought was once more set free in the eastern and western provinces, when only one result could follow, namely, a strong development of Liberalism.

The mountainous land and the majestic boundary of Old Ocean have made a hardy, plucky, and spirited people in Nova Scotia, New Brunswick, and Prince Edward Island. Their representatives are quite equal to anything we turn out in Ontario, and it requires very moderate vision to discern that intelligence, independence of spirit, and Liberalism in politics, will always characterize those eastern provinces.

And what is there to conserve, or make Conservatives of, in Manitoba or British Columbia, where there is literally nothing yet, and everything to create? It is true that the representatives from British Columbia have always shown strong partisanship; but, to me, it always appeared as merely personal and not political.

Thus I have no doubt whatever but that the present Liberal Government will be largely supported by all the provinces, and that when Parliament again meets it will possess a larger majority than the largest of the late Government in the Spring session, and that no necessity will arise for a general election before the usual time.

The people should exact a policy and measures from a Government, and support or oppose on the same.

Borrowed money has to be paid with interest. Industry and lands, to be profitable and entirely remunerative, require a circulation of money in ample quantity to make credit exceptional instead of general. Credit begets debt, and debt is the curse of mankind, checking woefully the material development of a country. It is the weapon with which the coarser minded men impoverish their superiors.

"The cart is before the horse" in the Canada system of industry, as, at present, production is under the heel of commerce. This is illogical, because production could be without commerce, but not commerce without production. The banks are purely mercantile, and their circulation of five or six dollars per head (of the population) is merely mercantile.

The Americans have twenty-eight dollars per head, and the English, in their specie, check system, and bank notes, have double the American amount.

The progress of a people, other things being equal, in wealth, comfort, health, happiness, intelligence, and even in increase of population, is exactly relative to the amount of the circulating medium called money.

The speediest process to obtain a proper money of production, instead of the present mercantile money, is for the constituencies to only elect representatives pledged to demand a national currency, a currency unaffected by the exigencies of banks and merchants.

Every man in the land who respects himself, and who deems liberal and even-handed political principles as essential to the country's well-being, should, for the time, acquiesce in the present change of Government, and not expect a full development of measures just at once. I recognize, myself, the rights of a minority: they have just as much interest in the county and country as any momentary majority.

Therefore, I address this to all the inhabitants of Welland, with my most respectful regards.

WM. A. THOMSON.

November 10, 1873.

APPENDIX B: MEMORIAL ARRANGEMENTS

OBITUARY NOTICES OF THE LATE WM. A. THOMSON,

A Member of the Parliament of the Dominion,

Representing the County of Welland in the

House of Commons of Canada

BORN IN WIGTOWNSHIRE, SCOTLAND, NOVEMBER 7, 1816

DIED AT GLENCAIRN, ONTARIO, OCTOBER 1, 1878.

"The memory of a life nobly rendered is immortal."

The late William A. Thomson.
We regret to have to announce the death of Mr. W.A. Thomson, late M.P. for Welland, a gentleman well-known in Canada, for his advanced views and enterprising spirit. The event was not unexpected, Mr. Thomson having been for some time in failing health. He

was compelled to relinquish his attendance in the House of Commons during the last session of Parliament from this cause, and for the same reason to decline to become a candidate at the recent general election. Mr. Thomson was a native of Wigtownshire, Scotland, where he was born in November, 1816. At the age of eighteen he came to America, and was for some years a resident of Buffalo, where he carried on business. He was a man of bold, speculative turn of mind, and identified himself with railway undertakings. The construction of the Erie and Niagara, and afterwards of the Canada Southern Lines, in the face of many – all but insuperable difficulties, having been largely the result of his determination, perseverance, and energy. Mr. Thomson was an unsuccessful candidate in the Reform interest for Niagara in 1867; and in 1872, on the death of the late Mr. Thomas Street,[95] he was elected – after a very severe contest – for the county of Welland. He was a pronounced free trader in sentiment, and held strong views on the questions of commercial credit, the currency, and banking. In the session of 1878 he spoke at length on the subject of Agricultural Banks, and was also engaged in promotion of railway enterprises in Manitoba. He was a large hearted, liberal man, of kindly and social sympathies, a loyal member of his political party, and true to his convictions. After an active and busy life, marked by many exciting incidents and controversies, he leaves behind him not a few sorrowing friends, but no enemies. – *Toronto Globe*, October 2nd, 1878.

The death of Mr. W.A. Thomson, which took place at his residence on the Niagara River on Tuesday morning, has called forth many expressions of regret here, as well as elsewhere in Ontario. He was one of the best known men in the lake shore counties and by his excellent social qualities, great energy and independent spirit, he had in the course of life gathered around him a host of attached friends. Here his name is inseparably associated with the Canada Southern Railway, and his persevering labors in connection with that great enterprise deserve the lasting gratitude of our people. He was one of a few men in the world who either find a way or make it, and as the successful promoter of this highway of commerce he encountered and overcame difficulties that would have overwhelmed any man of less genuine vigor and pluck. Great battles have been fought and won with one-third of the generalship Mr. Thomson displayed in that contest. It was a struggle of brains against capital, and in a mean money-getting age, brains won. The story of the struggle, if it be ever written, will form one of the most interesting chapters in the history of Canadian railways. Mr. Thomson was more than a railway promoter. His information was extensive, and there were few important subjects upon which he had not matured an opinion. He had thought very closely on the troublesome question of finance, and though laughed at by some people for his views thereon, no one can carefully read his essay on the Philosophy of Political Economy and deny his title to the rank of a philosophical inquirer after truth. He was a Liberal of the most pronounced type, and as such rendered the Government of Mr. Mackenzie[96] important and valuable service during the past five years. Mr. Thomson was born in Wigtownshire, Scotland, in 1816, and came to Canada in 1834. In partnership with his brothers, he carried on business as a merchant in the city of Buffalo for a number of years, but meeting with some reverses he returned to Canada and undertook construction of Erie and Niagara Railway, which he completed. In 1867 he was an unsuccessful candidate for Parliament in the burgh of Niagara, but was elected for Welland in 1872, upon the death of Mr. T.C. Street. He represented that constituency until the close of the last parliamentary term. The illness which had its fatal termination on Tuesday morning came upon him during the last session, and shortly afterwards – knowing that the hand of death was upon him – he resigned to the Welland Reform Association the trust which six years before they had committed to his keeping.

He leaves a wife, one son, and a number of daughters to lament his loss and to cherish his memory. - *St. Thomas Journal, October 4th, 1878.*

The news of the death of Mr. W.A. Thomson, formerly Dominion Member for Welland, which took place at his residence near Queenston early yesterday morning, will be received throughout the country with profound regret. The deceased gentleman had been ailing for some time past, and last session was compelled to leave Ottawa and return home. Mr. Thomson was universally recognized as a man of great energy and public spirit. It was his indominable perseverance that pushed through the Canada Southern Railway when many of those interested had given the scheme up as hopeless; and throughout an active business life, he was ever distinguished for the same pluck and clear sightedness. He was born in Wigtownshire in 1816, but it may be said that his whole life was spent on this side of the Atlantic. He paid much attention to the science of finance, and although his views were not shared in by the majority, he advocated them none the less vigorously. * * * In private life Mr. Thomson was a most estimable man, and his death will be deplored by a large circle of friends. - *Toronto Mail, Wednesday, October 2nd, 1878.*

On Tuesday the Hon. W.A. Thomson, formerly of this city, and recently a member of the Canadian Parliament, died at his home near Queenston, of Bright's disease of the kidneys.[97] The deceased was about 62 years old, having been born in Wigtownshire, Scotland, in 1816. He emigrated to America when eighteen years old, and settled in this city, where he entered into the hardware business. He was a man of large capacity and bold speculative turn of mind. He early identified himself with railway undertakings, and was the projector of the Canada Southern, which he carried to a successful completion in the face of all but insuperable obstacles. After Mr. Thomson took up his residence in Canada he ran for Parliament in the Reform interest of 1867 but was defeated. In 1872, however, he was elected a member for the county of Welland after a severe contest. He was a pronounced free-trader, and his views on currency and banking carried great weight. He was compelled to relinquish his attendance at the House of Commons during the last session, owing to failing health. Mr. Thomson was well known among our citizens, and made many warm friendships by his liberality, his large heartedness, and kindly sympathies. The deceased leaves a wife and eight children. The funeral will take place at noon today at St. Mark's Church, Niagara. - *Buffalo Express, Thursday Morning, October 3, 1878.*

Funeral of the late W.A. Thomson.

The remains of the late W.A. Thomson were interred on Thursday last. The place chosen for the purpose is a neatly laid out graveyard in the town of Niagara; and the spot, singularly quiet and retired under the shadows of the wall and of the overhanging foliage. It gives an idea of repose mournfully appropriate to the last resting place of a man engaged in life with large and lofty plans and aims for the benefit of his fellows, and wearied with the restless activity and close attention their execution required. Here the large, well-built, and manly frame which made W.A. Thomson a commanding figure in every crowd – as his active intellect made him a prominent citizen and a felt power in every community of which, for the time, he formed a part – will rest.

His form has vanished from sight, but the result of his wonderfully successful enterprises are still ours to enjoy, and the memory of his public deeds will be gratefully cherished by the people of South Western Ontario. In their midst he has left behind him a monument of a spirit of indominable perseverance, of daring public courage, of unconquerable will, of a power of accomplishment that is unique in the history of public works – a spirit that in all likelihood will never cease to perpetuate its good offices, nor to cause happiness and prosperity to flow from one end of the land to the other. The Canada Southern Railway was the most prominent of his schemes, but was by no means the only one. Of these many, however, not now.

At noon on the 3rd instant, leading citizens from Buffalo, St. Catharines, Hamilton, and Toronto, together with a large concourse of his friends in Welland and Lincoln, assembled at Glencairn, his family residence for the past dozen years, to pay to departed worth their last tribute of respect. The cortege moved from this beautiful country seat on the banks of the majestic Niagara – a home of blessed surrounding influences, magnificent in its very simplicity – at 12:30. The pallbearers were His Honor Judge Beckwith, of Buffalo; Judge Macdonald of Welland; Judge Lauder, of Lincoln; Dr. Campbell, President of the Ontario Medical Association, of Toronto; Mr. Russell, of Fort Erie; and Mr. McLachlin, of this town. The place of interment was six miles distant, and hundreds followed in their carriages, while others went forward by free train placed at their disposal by that quiet and considerate kindness of heart which has ever distinguished the General Manager of the Canada Southern Railway, Mr. W.K. Muir,[98] who was himself present to sympathize with the afflicted, and to join in the common tribute of respect to one who was for many years a valued co-laborer in railroad enterprise.

Dr. McMurray, of Niagara,[99] conducted religious services at the house, and the formal ceremonies in the cemetery.

At 3 o'clock the attendants dispersed, and the train returned with its load of saddened and solemnized hearts. - *St. Thomas Journal, October 8th, 1878.*

As a mark of their esteem for our late representative in Parliament, and to show their appreciation of the invaluable services rendered by him to the county, the Niagara Town Council, at a meeting on the 1st of October adopted the following resolution, which we are sure will be fully concurred in by the public of Welland County:

Resolved, That the members of this Council desire to record their deep regret at the death of their highly esteemed friend, Wm. A. Thomson, by which an irreparable loss has been sustained by the country at large, which is indebted to his untiring energy for the line connecting Lake Ontario at this point with the railway system of Canada and the Western States, as well as for other important services; and they tender their warmest sympathies to the bereaved family;

That a copy of the above resolution be transmitted to the family.

JOHN ROGERS   HENRY PAFFARD
Town Clerk   *Mayor*
Niagara Council, November 8th, 1878.
    Welland Tribune, Nov. 29, 1878.

Extract from Report of Proceedings of County Council of Welland, January Session.

Moved by Mr. Law, seconded by Mr. Hooker: That the members of this Council desire to record their sincere regret at the death of their late representative in the House of Commons of Canada - Wm. A. Thomson, Esq. - which sad event has been a severe loss to the country at large, and has likewise been the means of depriving the County of Welland of a most energetic and able representative, one whose recent efforts in behalf of the County in procuring from the Government a very valuable money concession were of practical value to this constituency, and deserve the gratitude of this Council. The country at large, and this County in particular, are indebted to our late representative's untiring energy for the construction of a really magnificent line of railway, running through the center of the latter, and connecting the railway system of the former with that of the United States, namely the Canada Southern Railway. And this Council beg to tender to the bereaved family their warmest sympathy in their affliction, and to express their sorrow for their loss in being deprived of a kind father and an affectionate and good husband.

That the Clerk will, without delay, forward a copy of this resolution, with the corporate seal attached, to the family at Glencairn. - Carried without a division. - *Welland Tribune, January 31st, 1879.*

A friend says of Mr. Thomson: "His character is one which it is a pleasure to recall, a pride to record, and a profit to imitate." A simple but substantial monument of granite from his native Scotland has been erected in Niagara beside the grave of the honored and lamented dead, with the following inscription:

Sacred to the Memory of

WILLIAM A. THOMSON,

Late Member for Welland, in the Parliament of Canada.

BORN IN WIGTONSHIRE, SCOTLAND,

November 7th, A.D. 1816

DIED AT "GLENCAIRN," ONTARIO,

Oct. 1st, A.D. 1878.

"The memory of a life nobly rendered is immortal."

Weep not for death,
'Tis but a fever stilled,
A pain suppressed, a fear at rest,
A solemn hope fulfilled.
The moonshine on the slumbering deep
Is scarcely calmer; wherefore weep?
    Weep not for death,
The fount of tears is sealed.
Who knows how bright, the inward light
To those shut eyes revealed?
Who knows what peerless love may fill,
The heart that seems so cold and chill.[100]

NOTES

1 This Introduction was written by a Thomson family relative. More likely than not, it was written by T. Kennard Thomson.

2 The Locofocos were a political faction, primarily in New York State, which opposed the Tammany Hall political organization, and aligned themselves with Andrew Jackson and Martin Van Buren. The Locofocos supported the abolition of the Second Bank of the United States, among other things.

3 Henry Burden (1791-1871) was a Scottish-born inventor and industrialist. He engaged in ferrous metals operations in Vermont and New York State. For further information, see Victor R. Rolando, "The Industrial Archaeology of Henry Burden & Sons Ironworks in Southwestern Vermont," Journal of Vermont Archaeology, Volume 8, 2007, pages 26-51.

4 The water works visited by William A. Thomson were the Fairmount Water Works, designed in 1812 by Frederick Graff.

5 The 1840 statue of George Washington by Horatio Greenough (1805-1852) made him look like a Greek god, and thus was controversial.

6 The painting General George Washington Resigning His Commission was painted by John Trumbull (1756-1843).

7 The painting Surrender of General Burgoyne was painted by John

Trumbull (1756-1843).

8 The painting <u>Baptism of Pocahontas</u> was painted by John Gadsby Chapman (1808-1889).

9 In 1894, Birmingham merged into Derby.

10 Blake Brothers developed and manufactured door locks, latches, casters, hinges, and other articles of hardware. One of the brothers was Eli Whitney Blake (1795-1886), nephew of Eli Whitney, who invented the cotton gin.

11 Trumbull's Gallery of Paintings was founded in 1832; it is the oldest university art museum in the Western Hemisphere. It was founded with John Trumbull's donation of more than 100 paintings pertaining to the American Revolution. It has evolved into the Yale University Art Gallery.

12 Rev. Jacob L. Clarke was Rector of Saint John's Episcopal Church in Waterbury, Connecticut.

13 The Collins Company was founded in 1826 near Canton, Connecticut. One of the founders was David C. Collins. The company introduced the first ready-to-use axes; previously, one could either purchase an unground axe and sharpen it, or purchase an axe from a local blacksmith. The company closed in 1966, but the brand name survives; Collins axes are still being made by Truper Herramientas in Mexico.

14 Monte Video was the Daniel Wadsworth estate on Talcott Mountain, a short distance west of Hartford. Talcott Mountain provides a spectacular view, but it is not the highest mountain in Connecticut. The highest elevation in Connecticut is on Mount Frissel, whose peak is in Massachusetts. The highest peak in Connecticut is Bear Mountain in Salisbury, Connecticut.

15 The Dramatic Line of packet ships was founded in 1836. Its ships were named after various figures connected with the theater. The <u>Roscius</u> was named after Quintus Roscius Gallus (ca. 126 B.C.E.-62 B.C.E.), a famous Roman actor. On September 1, 1860, the <u>New York Times</u> reported that the <u>Roscius</u> had been wrecked, but that all aboard had been rescued. At the time of William A. Thomson's eastbound trip in 1843, the captain of the <u>Roscius</u> was John Collins.

16 These lines were from "The Female Seductress," a poem by Henry Brooks, an Anglo-Irish poet and playwright (1703-1783).

17 He may be describing the appearance of Saint Elmo's Fire or luminescent plankton.

18 William A. Thomson called it a "hurricane." It was probably a bad storm, and not an actual hurricane, because the hurricane season is over by the end of November. The modern concept of a hurricane, with counterclockwise winds and an eye at the center, had not become established in 1843.

19 This riddle is most often attributed to Dean Peacock of Ely Cathedral. The answer to the riddle is the English crown. Between King William IV and Queen Victoria, the crown was kept overnight in a box called the "ark." Furthermore, if drawn out as a wire, the crown would stretch out about a mile.

20 Chiel is the Scottish word for "young man."

21 At that time, all of Ireland was under British rule. Thus, Belfast was in the "North of Ireland," because Northern Ireland did not yet exist.

22 Dulce is a variety of seaweed that grows on rocks on the Scottish and Irish coasts. It has a reddish color. In this incident, it was eaten raw. It is also used as an ingredient in Scottish soups.

23 General John Hamilton Dalrymple, 8th Earl of Stair (1771-1853). He served in the British Army and the British Parliament.

24 The Glencoe Massacre occurred in 1692, in the aftermath of the Jacobite Rising of 1689. About thirty people were killed.

25 The dissension arose when the Free Church of Scotland broke away from the Church of Scotland.

26 Charles Edwards Lester, The Glory and Shame of England (New York: Harper & Brothers, 1841).

27 Mary Stuart, Queen of Scots (1542-1587, reigned 1542-1567). Her second husband was Henry Stuart, Lord Darnley (1545-1567).

28 Joshua Scholefield (1775-1844) was an iron manufacturer, merchant, and banker in Birmingham. When Birmingham was enfranchised in the Reform Act of 1832, he was elected to Parliament, and served in Parliament until his death. (He was the father of William Scholefield, described in Chapter 13 below.)

29 Peregrine Wilton, "Nobody Is Missed," first published in <u>Blackwood's Edinburgh Magazine</u>, Volume 25, January-June 1829, page 71. Further information about Peregrine Wilton could not be located; Peregrine Wilton may have been a pseudonym. After this poem was published in 1829, it appeared in several other publications; William A. Thomson erroneously concluded that it was "unpublished."

30 Sir Walter Scott (1771-1832) was a prominent Scottish literary figure and public official. Among other things, he played a major role in establishing the historical novel as a literary genre.

31 These four lines are the second stanza of the familiar Anglican hymn "All praise to Thee, my God, this night," written in 1695 by Bishop Thomas Ken (1637-1711).

32 Mintons was an independent business from 1793 to 1868; it merged with Royal Doulton in 1968.

33 Copeland & Garrett operated under that name from 1833 to 1847; it operated as W.T. Copeland & Sons from 1847 to 1970; it merged into Spode Ltd. in 1970.

34 Samuel Alcock (1799-1848) operated as Samuel Alcock & Co. Eleven years after his death, his pottery closed due to bankruptcy.

35 William Davenport carried on the pottery of his father John Davenport (retired 1830) and his brother Henry (died 1835). William died in 1869; in 1887, the pottery was acquired by Burleigh Pottery.

36 The Stockport Viaduct was built in 1840. It carries the West Coast Main Line, a major north-south railroad line, across the River Mersey. The viaduct features 27 brick arches.

37 Muslin de laine is a thin worsted fabric, often having a printed pattern.

38 The Sandbach Crosses are a pair of Anglo-Saxon stone crosses, carved with various decorations, probably created in the Ninth Century; they are located in the Sandbach marketplace.

39 Oliver Cromwell (1599-1658) served as Lord Protector of the Commonwealth (1653-1658).

40 Water de Gray (circa 1180-1255) served, among other things, as Archbishop of York and Lord Chancellor of England.

41 Wesleyan Proprietary Grammar School in Sheffield opened in 1838. Its name was changed to Wesley College in 1844. In 1905, it merged with Sheffield Royal Grammar School to form King Edward VII School.

42 Scriptural passages relating to the refining of silver are Psalm 12:6, Ezekiel 22:18-22, Zechariah 13:9, and Malachi 3:3.

43 King William IV (1765-1837, reigned 1830-1837); Queen Adelaide (1792-1849).

44 Mary Stuart, Queen of Scots (1542-1587, reigned 1542-1567) was imprisoned by George Talbot, 6th Earl of Shrewsbury, at Chatsworth House several times, from 1570 onwards. She was lodged in rooms still known as the "Queen of Scots rooms."

45 Enceinte = pregnant.

46 William George Spencer Cavendish, 6th Duke of Devonshire (1790-1858).

47 William A. Thomson apparently had a very romantic view of life among the nobility in the Middle Ages. It never occurred to him that many noblemen at that time were robber barons.

48 The boar's head is the emblem of the Vernon family; the peacock is the emblem of the Manners family.

49 The Roman bath in Bakewell involves a warm spring; the water contains iron. In 1637, the Bakewell Bath House was built over the Roman bath.

50 Bakewell pudding is an English dessert consisting of a flaky pastry base with a layer of sieved jam and topped with a filling made of egg and almond paste.

51 The Parkgate Ironworks were established in 1823. The company has undergone many changes in technology and many changes in ownership since that time.

52 William Scholefield (1809-1867) was a son of Joshua Scholefield (described in Chapter 6 above). In December 1838, William Scholefield was elected the first Mayor of Birmingham, after a modern municipal government was created to replace a medieval manorial court. In 1847, he was elected to Parliament, and served until his death.

53 In Sir Walter Scott's Ivanhoe, a character says, "Yonder is Rotherwood, the dwelling of Cedric the Saxon."

54 Chance Brothers & Company, Ltd. commenced business in 1824. Over the years, it has manufactured a great variety of glass products. Its current name is Chance Glass Ltd.

55 The Birmingham Polytechnic Institution was founded in 1843, for higher education in scientific and other practical subjects. It closed down in 1853.

56 King Edward's School in Birmingham was founded by King Edward VI in 1552. Charles Barry (1795-1860) was a prominent English architect.

57 Birmingham Town Hall was built in 1834. It was modeled on the Temple of Castor and Pollux in the Roman Forum. It has always been a concert hall; it has never served as the Birmingham municipal building. The Birmingham City Council House serves as the Birmingham municipal building.

58 The organ in Birmingham Town Hall was installed in 1834. It has 6,000 pipes. The longest pipes are 32 feet long; for the first time in England, they were incorporated into the decorative case front.

59 I Corinthians 15:55.

60 Monument to Sarah Morley in Gloucester Cathedral, 1784.

61 George Whitefield (1714-1770) was a Methodist preacher. He was never a bishop; William A. Thomson must have been referring to someone else when he indicated that a bishop was born in the Bell Tavern.

62 A camera obscura is a darkened chamber in which the image of an object or landscape is received through a small opening, and focused in natural color on a facing surface, in an inverted orientation.

63 The Palace of Westminster, commonly known as the Houses of Parliament, had suffered a devastating fire in 1834. It was rebuilt in 1840-1876.

64 The Mansion House is the official residence of the Lord Mayor of London. It was built in 1739-1752.

65 The Guild Hall is the ceremonial and administrative center of the City

of London. It was built in 1411-1440.

66 Temple Bar is the monument at the western boundary of the City of London; beyond Temple Bar is the City of Westminster. When William A. Thomson visited London, Temple Bar was an ornamental Baroque arched gateway designed by Sir Christopher Wren. In 1878, it was removed, and subsequently replaced with a pedestal topped by a statue of a dragon.

67 William A. Thomson describes the Tower of London's armor collection and the Crown Jewels. The mint at the Tower of London had closed down in 1812, and the menagerie had closed down in 1835.

68 The British term "corn" refers to grain in general and wheat in particular.

69 Doctors' Commons was the establishment of the lawyers who practiced in courts based on civil (Roman) law, as distinct from English common law. These courts' jurisdiction included admiralty, probate, and ecclesiastical matters. Doctors' Commons ceased operations in the late Nineteenth Century.

70 The College of Arms, also called the Heralds' College, operates the English system of heraldry.

71 Lincoln's Inn (founded in 1422) is one of the four currently existing Inns of Court. Serjeants' Inn was dissolved in 1877.

72 At that time, there were two Vice Chancellors: Sir James Lewis Knight-Bruce (1791-1866) and Sir James Wigram (1793-1866).

73 The Court of Rolls has never existed, although there is a person called the Master of the Rolls.

74 Daniel O'Connell (1775-1847) campaigned for the rights of the Irish; in particular, equal rights for Irish Catholics and repeal of the Acts of Union which combined Great Britain and Ireland. The eight-page program for the event is entitled "Programme of the vocal music with the words of the glees, choruses, & c. selected for performance during the dinner given to Daniel O'Connell Esq. M.P. at Covent Garden Theatre on Tuesday, March 12, 1844."

75 Finger glasses = finger bowls.

76 Thomas Slingsby Duncombe (1796-1861) was a Member of Parliament. He supported the rights of Dissenters, Catholics, and Jews.

77 John Talbot, 16th Earl of Shrewsbury (1791-1852) was also Lord High Steward of Ireland, an office the Earls of Shrewsbury have held since 1446.

78 Louis Antoine Jullien (1812-1860) was a flamboyant figure in the musical world. He held spectacular masked balls at Covent Garden.

79 The Drury Lane Theater was built in 1660. When William A. Thomson visited London, he saw the theater as rebuilt in 1812.

80 Thomas Sheridan (1719-1788) and Edmund Kean (1787-1833) were prominent actors. The Kemble family was a family of prominent actors.

81 William A. Thomson mentioned the Elgin Marbles (acquired 1816) but did not mention the Rosetta Stone (acquired 1802).

82 When William A. Thomson visited Westminster Abbey, the two towers at the western end had been added about a hundred years before, so the building looked much as it does today.

83 The tomb of Mary Queen of Scots in Westminster Abbey is proximate to the tomb of Queen Elizabeth I. Elizabeth ordered the execution of Mary, but Mary has been the ancestor of every subsequent monarch.

84 The Stone of Scone was the Scottish coronation stone. After its capture by the English in 1296, it was fitted into the English coronation throne in Westminster Abbey. It was surreptitiously returned to Scotland in 1950, retrieved by the English in 1951, and permanently returned to Scotland in 1996.

85 The National Gallery was founded in 1824. The painters mentioned by William A. Thomson were Benjamin West (1738-1820) and Joshua Reynolds (1723-1792).

86 The Acadia was a Britannia-class wooden steam ship with side paddles. It was owned and operated by the Cunard Line. The Acadia was commissioned in 1840, sold to German interests in 1849, and scrapped in London in 1858.

87 Several sources identify him as Captain Alexander Ryrie.

88 Saint Mary Redcliffe in Bristol was named after Saint Mary and located atop a red cliff. Queen Elizabeth I called it "the finest, goodliest, and most famous parish church in England."

89 The church contains the grave (with an impressive memorial) of

Admiral Sir William Penn, father of the founder of Pennsylvania. William Penn, the founder of Pennsylvania, is buried in Buckinghamshire.

90 Gillespie's Hospital, Edinburgh, was founded by tobacco merchant James Gillespie (1726-1797).

91 In this context, a goose is a pressing iron for clothing, with a long curved handle.

92 The Pacific Scandal involved bribes to Canadian legislators, to influence the awarding of contracts for a transcontinental railroad. The recipients of these bribes tended to be members of the Conservative Party; this brought down the Conservative government in 1873.

93 Sir John A. Macdonald (1815-1891), of the Conservative Party, served as Prime Minister of Canada (1867-1873 and 1878-1891).

94 Sir George Cartier (1814-1873), of the Conservative Party, was for many years the most prominent politician in Quebec.

95 Thomas C. Street, Member of the Canadian Parliament, died in 1872, about 63 years of age. He was reputed to be one of the wealthiest men in Canada.

96 Alexander Mackenzie (1822-1892), of the Liberal Party, served as Prime Minister from 1873 to 1878.

97 Bright's disease, a kidney disease, was first described by the English physician Richard Bright in 1827. It was subsequently discovered that Bright's disease is actually a wide and diverse range of kidney diseases. Thus, Bright's disease is no longer used as a diagnostic category.

98 William K. Muir (1829-1892) was born in Kilmarnock, Ayrshire, Scotland. He held various management positions at various railroads.

99 The Venerable William McMurray D.D. (1810-1894) served as Rector of Saint Mark's Anglican Church, Niagara-on-the-Lake, Ontario, from 1857 to 1894.

100 From a poem "For Music" by Menella Bute Smedley (1820-1877). This poem was frequently used for memorial purposes in the late Nineteenth Century.